ADVANCE PRAISE

"Giles Lury reminds us again that behind a great brand there is normally a terrific story. In this collection of real life fables, we get both insight and entertainment – and provocations that will cause us to consider our brands and businesses with fresh eyes. Like a modern day minstrel, he allows us to benefit from the moral of fabulous tales of a huge array of brand and communication experience."

Patrick Cairns, CEO, Wessanen UK

"Giles serves up bite-sized chunks of wisdom that are delicious to chew on and leave you wanting more."

Phil Barden, Author of *Decoded. The Science Behind Why We Buy* and MD at Decode Marketing

"Giles' stories engage you and make you think about things from a different perspective; a good read that also helps me to do what I do better."

Alastair Paton Managing Partner, UK and Regional Director, EMEA, Signium

"Filled with little jewels of snackable content, From Ideas to Iconic Brands *amuses, informs and inspires."*
Kathy Leech. Executive Director, Corporate Brand and Advertising, Comcast

"There are so many stories behind brands, but to have such a variety, all imaginatively captured in one volume, complete with useable morals at the end of each one, is sheer joy for any brand marketer.
I am truly fascinated by brands and their stories, and Giles' latest collection is well-researched, wonderfully written, and full of curiosity – a must for any brand marketer!
It really makes you think about what you could do with your brand, as well as being thoroughly entertained at the same time."
Samantha L Fay, SVP Global Brand Strategy, Guinness World Records Ltd.

"Fantastic stories, which inform every aspect of brand thinking – entertaining and profound. I loved it!"
Miles Webber, Group Corporate Affairs & Sustainability Director at Land Securities

FROM IDEAS TO ICONIC BRANDS

Inspiring stories of 101 amazing brands that changed the world

GILES LURY

JAICO PUBLISHING HOUSE

Ahmedabad Bangalore Chennai
Delhi Hyderabad Kolkata Mumbai

Published by Jaico Publishing House
A-2 Jash Chambers, 7-A Sir Phirozshah Mehta Road
Fort, Mumbai - 400 001
jaicopub@jaicobooks.com
www.jaicobooks.com

Published in arrangement with
LID Publishing Limited
The Record Hall, Unit 304
16-16A Baldwins Gardens
EC1N 7RJ, London, UK

To be sold only in India, Bangladesh, Bhutan,
Pakistan, Nepal, Sri Lanka and the Maldives.

FROM IDEAS TO ICONIC BRANDS
ISBN 978-93-86867-89-6

Original English language edition published as
How Coca-Cola Took Over the World

First Jaico Impression: 2018

Printed by
Repro India Limited, Mumbai

DEDICATION

To my five 'brand extensions',
Rebecca, Jack, Callum, Theo and Ewan,
and the stories they are writing for themselves

TABLE OF CONTENTS

INTRODUCTION

Some people collect stamps, some collect coins, some collect football stickers; I collect stories.

In particular, I collect stories about brands.

I personally enjoy these stories, but I also use them in my job as a brand consultant to explain different principles and make specific points about marketing to my clients. I nearly always frame my points as stories, rather than just examples or case studies, as they are more interesting that way, and tend to be better remembered.

A while ago, I realized that I shouldn't just collect stories, but that I should write them down, tell them in my own words…and so that's what I did.

It was a number of years and a couple of false starts before I finally managed to compile enough stories and find the right publisher. But in the end I did that too.

My habit of collecting stories is now so ingrained that almost as soon as my first collection – *The Prisoner and the Penguin* – was published, I started gathering more. This book is the result of that work.

A Storybook Not a Textbook

Storytelling has always been used in marketing, and in recent years it has become a hot topic. Just about any brand worth its salt now talks about its 'storytelling', whether or not it is actually telling a story.

Numerous books and many more articles have been written about the art and science of storytelling. I identify seven uses for storytelling in marketing:

1. The brand narrative
   This is a means of presenting the organization/brand as a character and its role as a story. The brand Virgin, for example, has positioned itself as a 'white knight' riding to save the damsel (consumer) in distress. There are overlaps with brands as archetypes.
2. Did you know ...?
   This is when brands build emotional engagement by telling the little (true) stories about themselves: how the brand started, the origin of its name. These can be used to build emotional engagement.
3. Inspiring and cautionary tales
   The use of stories about brands as a training tool, to provide inspiration and/or instruction for the marketing team or broader organization. They can be used to show how employees should act, as a means of helping an organization perform better, or encourage people to think in different ways.
4. Up close and personal
   The telling of personal stories is another means of gaining emotional engagement. The parallels between the personal and the business situation are then highlighted to make a specific point – a technique used by CEOs and politicians worldwide.
5. Going metaphorical
   Here a fictional story is created that can act as a metaphor

for what has happened, or needs to happen, or as an entertaining expression of what your brand is doing. The 2013 animated short film *Scarecrow* to advertise American restaurant chain Chipotle Mexican Grill is a good example.

6. Meet your customer
   Stories, fictional but based on a true customer, are being used more frequently to personalize target segments and their beliefs and behaviours. They are a powerful way to bring to life target segments and touchpoints along any customer journey.
7. The 'story-tation'
   When did a PowerPoint slide last make you cry? Writing a presentation as a story is one way to try to avoid 'death by PowerPoint'. Using a narrative arc allows speakers to communicate points in a more engaging and memorable way.

My aim with *The Prisoner and the Penguin* was to combine inspiring and cautionary tales with entertainment. The aim of this new collection is the same: it's meant to be a story book and not a textbook. At best, I think these stories can be seen as fables with morals that can be applied to other brands in other markets.

Learning from Success

The Prisoner and the Penguin has been translated into Korean, Spanish, Thai and Japanese. Much to my delight it became a best-selling business book in Korea.

The Korean version featured only 60 stories (instead of the 76 in the UK edition) and was re-titled *Why Volkswagen Advertised the Broken Car.*

Choices, Choices

How did I select all the 101 tales in this book? There are literally millions of brands, and most claim to have stories.

It comes down to five criteria…

First of all, there is serendipity. Do I know the story? Did somebody suggest the story? Was I able to find out about the story? The first and very simple factor was awareness, in which case, to paraphrase Marlon Brando, it could be a contender.

Next: could it be a story, rather than a case study? Wherever possible I focus on one or two characters – in both senses of the words, people in a story and people who have some distinctive characteristics.

Then: is there a hook or twist? Does the story include something unexpected or outrageous? Do I think it will surprise and amuse my readers?

Fourthly, is there a moral that I can see? Is there a lesson marketers can take from the story? I have to feel there is something to be learned from it.

Lastly, there must be breadth to the collection. So while you will find one or two brands have more than one story, a huge variety of brands are mentioned.

Categories, categories

Following on from that last criteria, I then decided to categorize the stories into: branding, origins, naming and identities, marketing strategy, communications, innovation and repositioning.

This obviously reflected the breadth I was looking for, and hopefully provides you, dear reader, with some direction so you know either what you're going to get or where to look for what you want.

And finally

I can't finish without a few of the customary thank yous, which may be traditional but are none the less heartfelt.

Firstly, to family, friends, clients and colleagues for the kind words and encouragement, especially all those who actually read the book and even more to those who bought it!

Secondly to those who suggested, or indeed provided me with stories, they are always welcome.

Thirdly to Guy Chalkley who took on the mammoth task of doing all 101 illustrations and did such a great job.

Fourthly to the team at LID for their help, patience and guidance, thank you Martin, Sara, Caroline and Charlotte.

And finally to my wife and family who have put up with me writing away in the evenings and weekends without too much complaining.

BRANDING

Branding is an economic and social phenomenon.

Brands are tools for value generation in business. A brand's financial value is amongst a company's most valuable assets. In its 2016 list of best brands, Interbrand valued Apple at an incredible $178.1 billion.

John Stuart, one-time chairperson of Quaker, said: "If this business were to be split up, I would be glad to take the brands, trademarks and goodwill, and you could have all the bricks and mortar – and I would fare better than you."

Brands are also part of modern culture, referenced in songs, books and films. A strong brand has social 'meaning' – certain values and personality traits – that is consistent across consumers. It is this meaning that becomes a unit of social currency.

We may all have individual perceptions of these brands, but we also know the generally agreed characteristics and meaning of those brands. Sir Michael Perry, when chairperson of Unilever, said: "In the modern world, brands are a key part of how individuals define themselves and their relationships with one another… More and more, we are simply consumers… We are what we wear, what we eat, what we drive."

This section looks at stories that demonstrate the power of brands to change markets, and sometimes change the world.

1. HOW COCA-COLA TOOK OVER THE WORLD

On 25 May 1961, President Kennedy delivered his special message to Congress on urgent national needs. In it he expressed a concern that the United States was falling behind the Soviet Union in technology and prestige. He set the nation a challenge of landing a man on the Moon and returning him safely to Earth before the decade was out.

Just over eight years later, on 16 July 1969, a Saturn V rocket launched Apollo 11 from Kennedy Space Center in Florida. On board were three astronauts – Neil Armstrong, Michael Collins and Edwin 'Buzz' Aldrin.

Four days later, the Apollo Lunar Module Eagle landed successfully on the Moon. Just after 02:30 (UTC) on 21 July, Neil Armstrong opened the hatch and began his descent.

On stepping onto the Moon's surface, he spoke the now historic words: "That's one small step for (a) man, one giant leap for mankind."

The Command Module Columbia returned to Earth on 24 July and, after touching down (well, splashing down), the astronauts began 21 days of quarantine.

So it wasn't until 13 August that there was a parade in their honour in New York. As they entered Times Square, the three astronauts were greeted by a flashing sign which read "Welcome home to Planet Earth, home of Coca Cola".

Apollo 11 had successfully completed its mission. President Kennedy's objective had been accomplished.

And Coca-Cola had successfully staked its claim to being the most famous brand on Planet Earth, and soon after started to receive applications for the first bottling franchises on the Moon.

And the moral is, good PR can be the most effective and cheapest publicity. What more could your brand do with PR?

Footnote: Armstrong claims to have said "that's one small step for a man, one giant leap for mankind" when he first set foot on the lunar surface. The "a" is not clear in NASA recordings, but the audio and video links back to Earth were somewhat intermittent, partly because of storms near Parkes Observatory. More recent digital analysis of the tape by NASA revealed the "a" may have been spoken but obscured by static.

2. BROWNIE WISE – THE QUEEN OF TUPPERWARE

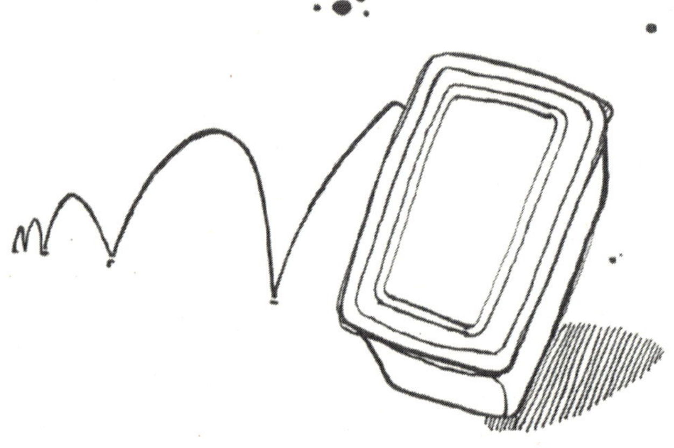

In 1956, the *Houston Post* reported that: "It has been estimated that Brownie Wise has helped more women to financial success than any other single living person." But who was Brownie Wise, and what was the brand upon which her, and so many other women's, success was built?

Brownie's story starts when she was born in rural Georgia and named after her big, brown eyes. Her parents divorced, and, as a teen, she travelled with her mother, who organized union rallies. It was on these trips that Brownie started giving speeches and soon proved to be an extraordinarily gifted and motivating orator. She "awed people", wrote her biographer Bob Kealing. "[They] were surprised that someone so young could deliver a speech like a pastor."

The next stage on her path to success started with a bad door-to-door salesman. When a Stanley Home Products salesman knocked on her door and proceeded to deliver a terrible sales pitch for cleaning supplies, Wise scoffed and said she could do better.

By coincidence, Stanley had just started experimenting with home parties as a sales method, so the salesman said, if Brownie was so sure of herself, why didn't she show them what she could do. She jumped at the chance and started selling Stanley products at parties. Before long, she was making enough money to quit her secretarial job.

Wise was blessed with the gift of the gab. She quickly started to rise through Stanley's ranks and was soon in management, hoping to ascend even higher. However, those aspirations were quashed at a meeting with Stanley's head, Frank Beveridge, who told her she'd never become an executive. Its halls were "no place for a woman," he said.

She was furious and started to look for other opportunities. It was a near-accident at a sales meeting that was to give her inspiration. One of her co-workers had seen some plastic storage tubs gathering dust in a department store and decided to bring them in. At first Wise didn't think they were anything special, but when she accidentally knocked a bowl off the table, it bounced instead of breaking, and the contents remained safe inside. Brownie saw the potential there and then.

The brand was Tupperware and, looking at it more closely, Brownie could see it looked attractive, came in attractive pastel colours and flexible shapes, but, above all, it was extremely functional. Convinced of its potential, Wise left Stanley, and in 1949 started throwing parties to sell Tupperware. It was a move that was to spark a mini revolution: Tupperware didn't just help extend the life of leftovers, it was to become a career maker for Brownie and millions of other women.

Many of the women who came to Wise's parties were convinced not only to buy the products, but to become Tupperware salespeople themselves.

Brownie quickly amassed outstanding sales, but, equally importantly, she started to build her team of saleswomen who in turn built their own networks. Soon, other Tupperware parties were taking place across the country. Wise's team in Detroit was selling more Tupperware than most department stores. This attracted the attention of Tupperware Corporation founder, Earl Silas Tupper.

He offered her a promotion: distribution rights for the entire state of Florida. In the spring of 1950, she moved south with her son and mother.

However, things didn't go as smoothly as she hoped: there were disputes over turf with other distributors. But what annoyed her most was that she was constantly contending with botched orders, shipping delays and product shortages.

In March of 1951, Wise had had enough. She called Tupper in a fury and demanded action – this was hurting not just her bottom line, but also his. The next month, the two met at a conference on Long Island, and Wise explained her belief in the power of parties where people could touch Tupperware, squeeze it, drop it and seal it in the company of trusted friends or neighbours. With regard to growing the business, her suggestion was radical: ditch department stores altogether and focus entirely on throwing home parties.

Tupper took the advice, and the day after their meeting he created a new division for home parties and asked Wise to be the general manager. The new approach saw Tupperware sales rocket: wholesale orders exceeded $2 million in

1952. Tupper increased her salary to $20,000 and, on her birthday in 1953, he presented her with a gold-dyed palomino horse. He also gave her the freedom to do practically whatever she wanted.

Wise started travelling the country recruiting, presiding over sales conferences, announcing contests and doling out prizes as an incentive – including, sometimes, her own clothes.

For many women in the 1950s, the beauty of selling Tupperware at parties was that it allowed them to be employed without appearing to challenge their husbands' authority, or the status quo of a very male-dominated world. Wise embraced the spirit of female entrepreneurship wholeheartedly: she wrote a newsletter called *Tupperware Sparks*, published a primer called *Tupperware Know-How*, and had a 52-minute film, *A Tupperware Home Party*, made as a training tool.

Wise had effectively become the face of Tupperware. In 1954, she was the first woman to appear on the cover of *Business Week*. The magazine's profile was glowing to say the least. It credited Wise and her sales technique with Tupperware's estimated $25 million in retail sales.

And the moral is that brands can drive change, not just in business but society too. What change will your brand be driving?

Footnote: Unfortunately, the *Business Week* article sowed the seeds of discontent between Tupper and Wise. Tupper felt its focus on Wise seemed to downplay his role as president. He sent a note to Wise: "However good an executive you are, I still like best the pictures ... with TUPPERWARE!" Not surprisingly their relationship started to deteriorate and, in 1958, Tupper fired Wise. After a heated legal battle, she received only $30,000 as a settlement. She had no stocks in the company.

Wise tried starting new companies but never achieved the same success she had with Tupperware. She ended up leading a quiet life, with her horses, pottery and her son until she died at her home in 1992.

3. GO ON: ANNOY YOUR CUSTOMERS, IT'S GOOD FOR BUSINESS, IT'S GOOD FOR THE WORLD

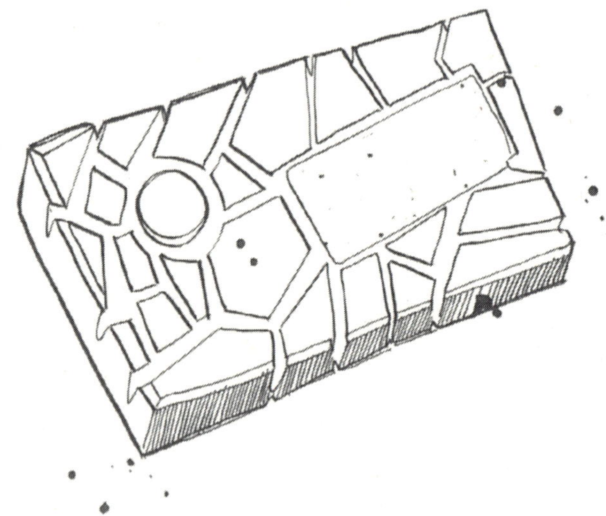

Tony's Chocolonely goes out of its way to annoy some of its customers.

Most chocolate bars are divisible into equal parts. People like the uniformity. It is easy to break off equal parts for yourself, or to ensure everyone gets the same sized piece when you're sharing a bar with friends.

Yet in 2012, Tony's Chocolonely, a Dutch-based chocolate company, deliberately introduced their unequally divided bar.

Not surprisingly they got comments and complaints. But the unequally divided bar continues. Tony's isn't being different just for the sake of being different, it is doing it for a reason. A reason linked to the very heart of its brand.

Tony's is a brand with a mission.

As its website explains, Tony's is "crazy about chocolate, serious about people – A 100% slave-free chocolate industry – that's our goal. It's the reason we created Tony's Chocolonely. And it's our mission to make other people as passionate about 100% slave-free chocolate as we are".

Set up by Maurice Dekker, a TV producer, and originally fronted by journalist Teun van de Keuken, it was the brand that arose out of their campaigning programmes. Programmes that highlighted the continuing child exploitation, and even slavery, in the chocolate industry in West Africa.

The first bars were part of a programme storyline with van de Keuken following the whole supply chain from bean to bar to demonstrate that a slave-free chocolate bar could be made. The first batch sold out within an hour of coming on to the market, so Dekker decided to start a company.

The brand name combines the anglicized version of "Teun" – Tony – and his "lonely" search for slave-free chocolate.

Another difference is the use of colour. Dekker recalls: "How was I to know that red is the code for pure chocolate and blue is for milk? I was ignorant of the whole industry and red to me is a colour to raise awareness, a signal. And that's what the first Tony's Chocolonely's milk chocolate bar was about. Raising the signal, the red flag."

The unequally divided bar comes from the same sort of thinking. It is unequally divided as it represents the unequally divided chocolate industry. In fact, if you look closely at the design, you can see the outlines of the chocolate-producing nations of West Africa – Cote d'Ivoire, Ghana, Togo and Benin, Nigeria and Cameroon.

Tony's aim was to make its customers stop and think about the chocolate they were eating, and to remember the inequalities within the chocolate-making supply chain.

Tony's is still getting complaints. But rather than change, the company is just happy to have a valid excuse to tell its story again.

And the moral is that you can build your brand right into your products. How can your product or service tell your story for you?

4. A ROAD SO BAD THEY JUST HAD TO BUY IT

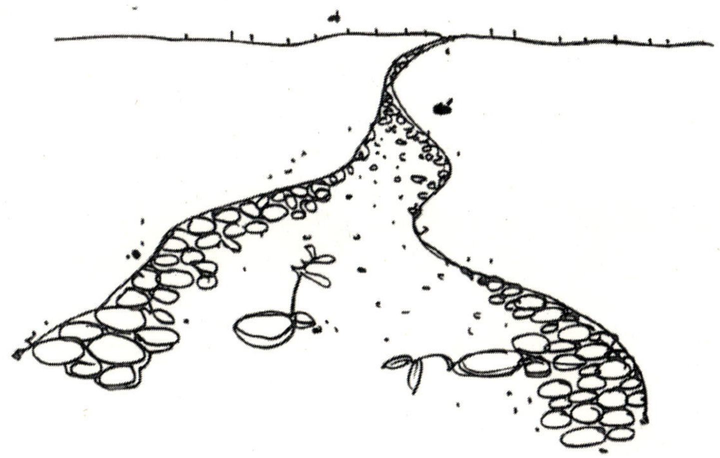

At Ehra-Lessien, 12-and-a-half miles from the German city of Wolfsburg, Volkswagen has a testing facility. It covers some 2,718 hectares and over 62 miles of test tracks.

There is a high-speed track with a straight that runs for approximately 5.5 miles. The banked corners at both ends allow for a high entry and exit speed to and from the straight. It was here in July 2010 that a Bugatti Super Sport, a car with 1,200 bhp (890 kW), recorded the production car world speed record at an average of 267 mph.

There is a cross-country track where the terrain tests suspension, tyres and steering to the limit, which is perfect for trying out new 4x4s. There are salt-water crossings which can short electrical systems and leave rust-forming deposits in exposed parts of any bodywork. There are skid pans across which test drivers hurl cars at breakneck speeds. There is even a 'mountain' with gradients of up to 32% and hairpin bends as hairy as any in the Alps.

There are, however, also some urban driving tracks, including an incredibly lumpy, bumpy cobbled street full of potholes, just like you might find in a nearby village … or rather exactly like the one you would have found in the nearby village of Hehlingen.

The reason being that a number of the people who worked at Ehra-Lessien used to drive through Hehlingen on the way to work. Two of them were discussing the dreadful state of the main road there, and how it was potentially lethal when snowy or icy.

Unbeknown to them, their conversation was overheard by a senior manager at the facility. He jumped in his car to see if the road was really as bad as they said. Arriving, he found that it was…and it was just what he wanted.

Volkswagen opened negotiations with the local council to 'buy' the road, ultimately replacing it with a nice, new, smooth tarmac surface, and building a community swimming pool as a thank you.

Volkswagen transported the old road, stone by cobbled stone, to Ehra-Lessein, where the company re-laid it complete with ruts and pot-holes.

That was in 1967, and ever since the road has been meticulously maintained in the same dreadful condition, since Volkswagen still believes that it needs the worst conditions to produce the best cars.

And the moral is that it pays to go to extreme lengths to test the quality of your brand. How far will you go to prove your brand?

5. THE BRAND BUILT ON A HANDSHAKE

When he was only six-years-old, an already sports-mad Mark McCormack was struck by a car as he crossed the street in his home-town of Chicago. He fractured his skull. The accident set in motion a series of events that was to change not only McCormack's life, but also the whole future of sports and entertainment marketing.

When he finally recovered from his injuries, his doctors advised against playing any contact sports, so his father, Ned, bought him a set of golf clubs and encouraged him to take up the game.

Golf was soon his passion. He played on the golf team at Virginia's College of William & Mary, and qualified as an amateur for the US Open of 1958.

It was, however, while playing for William & Mary that McCormack first met the young Wake Forest golfer who would change his life. The young golfer's name was Arnold Palmer.

After Wake Forest, Palmer headed off for a career in professional golf. After William & Mary, Mark headed off first to Yale Law School, and then to a law firm in Cleveland. They kept in touch and a friendship was born.

In 1960, Mark had an idea. He could see the rising value of athletes, and in an era when golf's popularity was rising and televised sport was emerging, he felt he had an opportunity to represent and maximize the earnings of golfers.

Meeting Palmer again, he pitched his idea: a company that would serve as personal business manager for professional golfers.

"I'll be your Clifford Roberts," Palmer recalled McCormack saying. Roberts served as President Eisenhower's ultimate inner-circle man, adviser and protector, friend and counsellor, through good times and bad. And President Eisenhower trusted him implicitly.

Palmer took to the idea immediately. It would allow him to concentrate on his golf while someone he could trust looked after his business issues.

Palmer later said: "[McCormack] asked for a contract. I said, 'We don't need a contract. We'll just shake hands, and you've got a client'. That kind of shook him up a little, but he did it."

In his book *A Golfer's Life*, Palmer would reflect: "There was no contract between us because Mark knew my word was my bond, and there would be no turning back on my part. The same was true of him, and those stories that you've heard about us never formalizing our business relationship in printed legalese, are true."

So down to business they got, and in Palmer's first two years with McCormack, his endorsement earnings grew from $6,000 to $500,000. Palmer won the Masters, but also played golf with presidents, and promoted Pennzoil and Hertz rental cars. It was the kind of success that the golf world (and indeed the entire sports world) hadn't seen before.

Others wanted some of what Palmer was achieving, and McCormack signed Jack Nicklaus and Gary Player, helping to create and then aggressively market what was christened "The Big Three".

McCormack and his now rapidly growing company, International Management Group (IMG), soon branched out into other sports. New clients included Rod Laver, Bjorn Borg and Jimmy Connors of tennis; and Pelé, the world's most famous footballer. Nick Faldo, Greg Norman, Pete Sampras, Tiger Woods and other legends would come later.

McCormack also backed his belief in the potential value that could be created by marrying sports, his famous clients and television. He started a television division called Trans World International. It was another immediate success, and some of its most popular programmes included *Big 3 Golf*, *American Gladiators*, and *Battle of the Network Stars*, as well as shows promoting *Barclays Premier League* soccer, the *ASP Tour*, and *World's Strongest Man* competitions.

Trans World International also negotiated television rights deals for the All England Tennis Club, the British Open, the NFL, Major League Baseball, and the NBA.

Perhaps not surprisingly in 1990, *Sports Illustrated* named McCormack the "Most Powerful Man in Sports".

Following his death in 2003, *Business Age* said of him: "McCormack invented the sports business. It was he who first realized that, within the golden triangle of sport, sponsorship and television, lay vast wealth, just waiting to be tapped."

And that wealth was built on a simple handshake.

And the moral is, brands are built on trust. What have you done to demonstrate you deserve the trust of your customers?

6. THE GANGSTER, THE LETTER AND THE DANDY CAR

Clyde Barrow and his lover and partner-in-crime, Bonnie Parker, are infamous for their two-year robbery spree which ran across the central United States and started in 1932. That 'spree' included at least a dozen bank robberies and numerous raids on small stores and rural gas stations. Bonnie, Clyde and their gang are believed to have killed at least nine police officers and several civilians during this period.

During 1932, 1933 and the early part of 1934, they evaded capture, and many people believe that two of the reasons for their continued freedom were Clyde's skill as a driver and the cars he drove.

Clyde's car of choice was the Ford V-8.

It offered both the speed and comfort the pair wanted. The V-8's over-head valve engine helped Clyde out-manoeuvre and out-run many of the less powerful police cars that attempted to follow him. Additionally, living a life on the run meant that Clyde and Bonnie spent days, and even weeks, at a time in their car, often sleeping in them at night so the extra comfort was equally appreciated.

Clyde was certainly a fan, and on 10 April 1934 he put pen to paper and wrote a letter to Henry Ford. It read:

Tulsa Okla
10th April
Mr. Henry Ford
Detroit Mich

Dear Sir:

While I still have got breath in my lungs I will tell you what a dandy car you make. I have drove Fords exclusively when I could get away with one. For sustained speed and freedom from trouble the Ford has got every other car skinned and even if my business hasn't been strictly legal it don't hurt anything to tell you what a fine car you got in the V8.

Yours truly,
Clyde Champion Barrow

The letter arrived at Henry Ford's office on 13 April 1934 where it was stamped "RECEIVED" by his secretary's office.

Just over a month later, on 23 May, the notorious couple were ambushed by state troopers and local police at Bienville Parish, Louisiana, and died in a hail of over 100 bullets.

The car they were driving was a stolen Ford V8.

The letter is on display at the Henry Ford Museum in Dearborn, Michigan.

And the moral is, the effects of good customer feedback can be multiplied through exploiting PR opportunities. How could you make more of your positive customer feedback?

7. JUST A SMILE AND A FEW DROPS OF CHANEL NO 5

There are many versions of this quote which seems to have first appeared in *Life* magazine on 7 April 1952.

Marilyn Monroe, then just 26-years-old, was asked: "What do you wear to bed?" And her reply, according to different sources was: "What do I wear to bed? Why, Chanel No 5, of course;" alternatively: "Just a few drops of Chanel No 5;" or maybe – my personal favourite: "Nothing but Chanel No 5 and a smile."

A year later in 1953, Monroe was photographed in bed for *Modern Screen* magazine, and, although the photos weren't published at the time, a bottle of Chanel No 5 can clearly be seen on her bed stand, which seemed to confirm the gist of the quote.

Then, in 1983, a long-lost sound-recording was rediscovered, which at least confirmed the truth of the original story.

The audio clip features the then *Marie Claire* editor-in-chief Georges Belmont interviewing Monroe in 1960 for her film *Let's Make Love*.

In her signature breathless voice, Marilyn can be heard saying: "You know, they ask me questions. Just an example: 'What do you wear to bed? A pyjama top? The bottoms of the pyjamas? A nightgown?' So I said, 'Chanel No 5,' because it's the truth ... and yet, I don't want to say 'nude'. But it's the truth!"

The sound clip was subsequently used by Chanel for a TV campaign featuring footage of the actress in a variety of situations including walking into a premiere, dancing, and on vacation.

And the moral is, celebrity endorsement can be a powerful tool to build your brand. Who and how would you like to endorse your brand?

8. TELL THEM TO GO AND DO SOMETHING ELSE

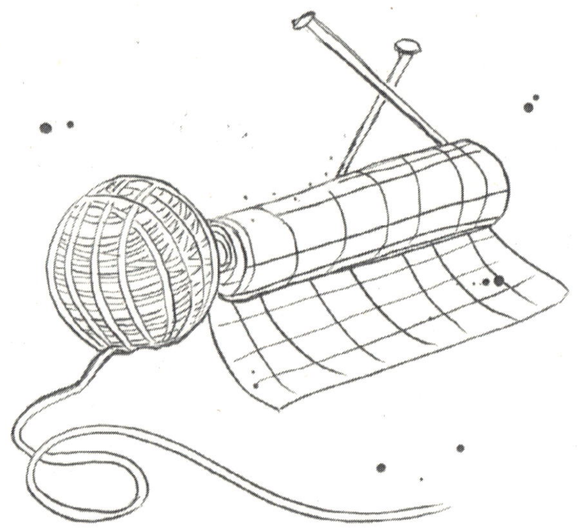

Most companies don't have a mission statement that explicitly states their aim is to get you doing something other than what the brand is about, but then Pinterest isn't most companies.

Its origins can be traced back to Des Moines in the early noughties when Ben Silbermann abandoned his long-held plans to follow his parents and both of his sisters to become a doctor. Instead, inspired by entrepreneurs like George Eastman of Walt Disney, he decided he should to get into business.

By chance, he was put in a company's IT group, simply because that's where there were openings. Amid the monotony of preparing spreadsheet after spreadsheet, he found himself reading *TechCrunch*, and as he told the Alt Summit in a speech in 2012: "I remember I had this feeling that this was the story of my time and I was in the wrong place."

Not long after he saw the movie about Steve Jobs and Bill Gates, *Pirates of Silicon Valley*, he decided that he needed to go west to be close to people who could inspire him.

Ben got a job at Google in customer support because, as he recalls: "I was more excited than the previous applicant." However, the job wasn't very different from his previous one; it involved analysing lots of data and making product design recommendations. It was basically preparing lots of spreadsheets all over again. Ben wanted to make products but Google didn't seem interested. He started complaining. Finally, his girlfriend said, "stop complaining and just go do it." Looking back, Ben sees this as a turning point and is eternally grateful to her: "If you're really lucky in life you have someone to call you out on your own bullshit."

Though at first it did seem that Ben's timing was off: "A week later, the entire economy collapsed," he recalled, and the friends who were going to join him felt that maybe their jobs at Google weren't so bad after all.

So Ben teamed up with a pal from college who was living in New York, Paul Sciarra, and they came up with a product called Tote, which Ben describes as "a catalogue that was on the phone."

While the concept was in many ways cutting edge, "everything seemed really hard. We couldn't get money. Apps had just been released so the approval process was taking months," Ben said.

Finally, their luck changed and one investor came through with a cheque. Ben took this opportunity to call those investors who'd said no previously: "You're going to miss out, this is a hot deal." It worked and they got more investment.

While Tote was moderately successful Ben and Paul were developing another idea. "I'd always thought that the things you collect say so much about who you are." Ben says his childhood bug collection is really "Pinterest 1.0".

Then on a visit to New York, Ben met a friend of a friend, Evan Sharp. They talked about the Pinterest concept. Ben remembers, "it was like he was the only one who understood what I was saying." Ben asked Evan to join them, and he is now credited as the third co-founder of Pinterest.

The very first 'pin' was put on the site in January 2010. It was picture of a Valentine's Day present Ben was thinking of buying his girlfriend.

Ben sent details of his new venture to all his friends in California, but the reaction wasn't quite what he'd hoped – "actually, no one got it."

Well that wasn't exactly true, users began to grow. Though Ben reckons that most early users came from Des Moines: "I suspect because my Mom was telling all her patients."

Then in May 2010, a woman named Victoria helped organize a programme called *Pin It Forward* – a virtual chain letter where bloggers would exchange pinboards about what home meant to them. It was to prove a tipping point.

Suddenly people started using Pinterest in ways Ben, Paul and Evan hadn't expected. One of the unexpected early boards was "Things That Look like the Deathstar" which included pictures of old teapots, puffball skirts and all manner of vaguely spherical things.

Victoria, who is now the company's community manager, organized the first Pinterest meet-up, and, looking back, Ben remembers thinking "that was the moment where I was like; 'We've got it.'"

And indeed they had, the brand went from strength to strength.

Nine months after the launch the website had 10,000 users.

The launch of an iPhone app in early March 2011 brought in more downloads than expected, and on 16 August of that same year, *Time* magazine listed Pinterest in its "50 Best Websites of 2011" article.

According to *Experian Hitwise*, the site became the third-largest social network in the United States in March 2012, behind Facebook and Twitter.

And while the company sees itself as "the place to plan the most important projects in your life", the brand's mission "is not to keep you online, it's to get you offline. Pinterest should inspire you to go out and do the things you love".

And the moral is, the best brands realize that they are only a small part of their users' lives. How do you make sure you don't over-estimate the loyalty of your users?

9. THREADLESS NOT CLUELESS, THE BRAND INSPIRING AWESOMENESS

"Threadless was never intended to be a business. When Jacob De Hart and I started out, it was just a hobby, a fun thing to do for the other designers we were friends with." So says co-founder Jake Nickell in his book on the birth and development of their brand.

The Threadless story begins in 2000 when Jake entered and won a competition on dreamless.org. The competition was to design a t-shirt for a New Media Underground Festival that was being held in London in November that year.

Jake's winning design was never printed, and he didn't even receive any prize money. However, the prize he did receive was an idea. He thought: "It would be fun to have an on-going competition where people could always submit t-shirt designs, and we would print the best ones."

Jake contacted his friend Jacob, who loved the idea, and Threadless was started about one hour later when the two friends posted their first call for entries on the dreamless.org forum.

They got nearly 100 entries and decided to pick 5 winners.

Committing $500 each to cover the cost of printing 24 of the 5 designs plus lawyer fees to help them incorporate the business, they then built a website through which they would sell the shirts.

Printing was done by Jacob's aunt, who happened to be a screen printer.

They priced the shirts at $12 and sold out quickly. The boys had their first success and even made some money: 24 x $12 = $1,440-$1,000 costs = $440 profit!

However, any money they made was ploughed back into the business, setting a precedent for their early years. "For the first two years of Threadless, every penny we made from selling tees went into printing more tee designs. We didn't even take a salary or cut of the sales," says Jake.

Instead, and in keeping with their philosophy, they spent their own time building up a community. The choice of winning tees was changed to customer voting, and Jake started posting news of the Threadless contests on any and every design website he could find. New batches of t-shirts were at first printed every couple of months, but soon became more and more frequent.

Threadless was still a hobby, and Jake and Jacob held down other web developer jobs for a living. But it grew fast, and by 2002 the community was 10,000-strong and sales were $100,000.

In 2004 when sales reached $1.5 million and new designs were being printed every week, the pair decided to quit their other jobs and concentrate on the brand.

Business boomed growing to $6.5 million, but the commitment to the community ethos continued. "Threadless is a community of people first, a t-shirt store second ... The best thing we did is to trust our community. To constantly ask them for advice, to show them we are listening, and to change things based on what the community is feeling. We also wholly invest ourselves in being members," says Jake in his book.

Even when the pair recruited professional help and Jake gave up the CEO role, he continued as CCO – chief community officer.

Interviewed by marketing consultant Jay Baer, Jake explained the significance of this on-going commitment and how they strive to maintain it.

"I think the values we have that have created the culture here are very important to the success. So now ...when new people are brought in... it's just really important to make it clear what Threadless is all about. We have a mission statement to "Inspire Awesomeness", and we have a bunch of internal things that we do to help make sure everyone's on the same page about it all. We do monthly awesome parties, host DIY days where anyone in the company can basically work on anything, anyone in the company can give anyone else in the company a bonus, etc... There are a ton of things we do!"

So it sounds like Jake and Jacob's original intention of it being "a fun thing to do" still holds true.

And the moral is, the best brands build communities, not just customers. What are you doing to build a community around your brand?

10. EVERY BUILDING TELLS A STORY

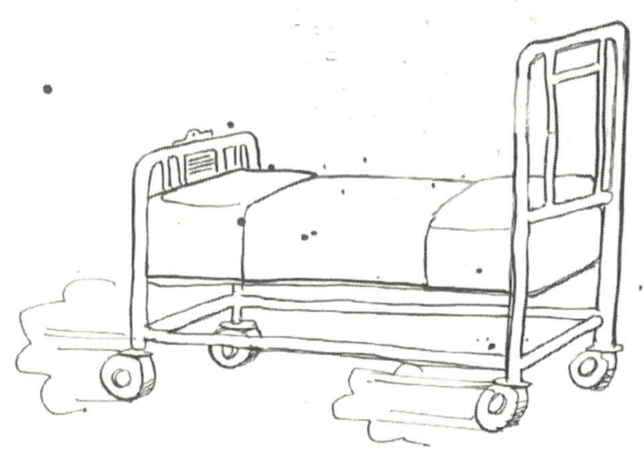

In a recent interview, head of Disney's global operations, Andy Bird, reiterated what's been at the core of the Disney brand since it began. "Storytelling is what the company is built on, and where we spend most of our energy."

But Disney doesn't just tell stories, it is made of stories: even its buildings have stories attached to them.

For example, take Disney's animation studio – a three-storey adobe-coloured building in Los Angeles whose corridors are covered with everything from rough sketches of Mickey Mouse and Pinocchio, to the computer-aided perfection of *The Lion King* and *Frozen*.

Walt Disney and his brother Roy used the profits from their 1937 film *Snow White and the Seven Dwarfs* to pay for its construction, but the venture was fraught with risk.

With one eye on the potential future, they insisted on roomy corridors — wide enough for hospital trolleys to be pushed through them with ease.

Why hospital beds?

"Roy thought that if things didn't work out, they could always sell the building to the hospital next door," said Andy Bird.

And the moral is, the best brands have a plan B. What will you do if your first plan doesn't succeed?

11. AN UNCOMFORTABLE VISION

Every spring, in every UK John Lewis store, every partner – as employees are known – stops and gathers on the shop floor, in the office or in the warehouse. They watch one of their colleagues open an envelope. On a single sheet is printed a number. That number represents the percentage of their salary that each and every one of them will receive as an annual bonus. Not surprisingly the event is nearly always greeted with a cheer.

This practice of equally sharing a proportion of the firm's profits can be traced back, not quite to John Lewis, but to Spedan Lewis his oldest son.

John Lewis was born in Somerset, England, and became an orphan at the age of seven. He was subsequently brought up by an aunt, Ann Speed. In 1864 he opened a small drapery shop, John Lewis & Co, at 132 Oxford Street in London. It flourished, so John expanded and the premises were rebuilt in the 1880s to form an all-encompassing department store.

Now married, John's first son was born in 1885 and was named in honour of his aunt – Spedan. At 19, Spedan went to work in the store, and on his 21st birthday his father gave him a quarter-share of the business.

It was then that Spedan realized that he, his father and his younger brother Oswald earned more from the business than all of the other employees put together. It was something that made him feel very uncomfortable.

In 1909, Spedan had a serious horse-riding accident which meant he would not work again for nearly two years. However, during the time he spent recuperating, he clearly brooded on the inequality of the situation and developed a plan to revolutionize the business. His vision was for a business where success should be measured by the happiness of those working at it, and by its good service to the general community.

When he finally returned to work – now running his father's second store, Peter Jones in Sloane Square – he started to turn his vision into reality. He shortened the working day, started a work committee, and increased paid holiday time. He wanted work to be something to live for as well as something to live by. While his ideas are said to have caused a rift with his father, they appeared to work as profits increased.

After the death of his father in 1928, Spedan assumed control of the Oxford Street store too. In 1929, he officially formed the John Lewis Partnership, and began the distribution of profits among its employees.

He completed the move towards employee-ownership in 1950, transferring control of the entire business to its employees.

Spedan Lewis resigned as chairman in 1955, but the legacy of his vision lives on.

And the moral is, the best brands strive to deliver something other than shareholder value. What is your vision of your brand?

12. NAUGHTINESS IN THE NOUGHTIES – WHAT HAPPENED WHEN VIRGIN TURNED 18

Back in the early 1980s, Richard Branson was best known for Virgin Records. He signed Mike Oldfield, whose Tubular Bells LP had been turned down by most of the established record labels. Its subsequent worldwide success was the basis on which the Virgin record label was built. It went on to sign major names like The Sex Pistols and The Rolling Stones.

In 1984, much to the horror of his fellow directors, Richard announced that he wanted to take on the airline industry and launch a high quality, value-for-money carrier that would begin operating within three months.

Virgin burst onto the traditionally staid air travel scene, introducing a series of innovations for business class passengers, and bringing a fresh, bold, bright, anti-establishment attitude.

In 1992, Richard sold Virgin Music to Thorn EMI and invested the proceeds into Virgin Atlantic to fund further innovations and further improvements to the service. Virgin shook up the industry and won many hearts and minds.

As the noughties arrived, the young upstart of an airline finally became an adult: Virgin was officially 18 in 2002. This was an occasion for celebration, but also worry – was the brand getting old and starting to lose its edge, its naughtiness?

So the marketing team decided to talk to staff and find out how they were bringing the Virgin attitude to life with passengers.

They heard many great tales, but one that really stood out was about chocolate desserts.

Susie (name changed) was working on the overnight flight from Heathrow to JFK, and decided to have a little harmless side-bet with her fellow stewardess, Annie (name also changed). They decided to see who could get the most passengers to take the chocolate dessert.

Just before the two stewardesses started to push their trolleys down the aisles, Susie took out one of the chocolate desserts, stuck her finger into it, and smeared some of it down her right cheek and towards her lips.

Leaving the gooey mess there, she approached the first passenger: "Can I tempt you with some dessert?" she asked politely, and then, just as he looked up, she added – with maybe just a hint of coquettishness in her voice: "I can personally recommend the chocolate."

Whatever the passenger had been going to say was immediately forgotten and instead he asked for the chocolate dessert as, perhaps not surprisingly, did the next passenger and the next, till Susie had run out of her stock of chocolate desserts.

Annie came back with half of hers left, well and truly beaten.

And the moral is that the best brands stay true to their core beliefs. What are the principles that your brand rests on (A principle isn't a principle until it costs you money)?

Footnote: A couple of years later, a consultant who had heard Susie's story was working with BA and asked the HR team what would have happened if one of their stewardesses had deliberately smeared a bit of chocolate dessert down her face and gently encouraged passengers to try it. The response: "She would have faced a disciplinary action and could have been fired", which just proves that both brands are well defined and quite clearly differentiated.

13. THE BRAND IS MIGHTIER THAN THE BUSINESS

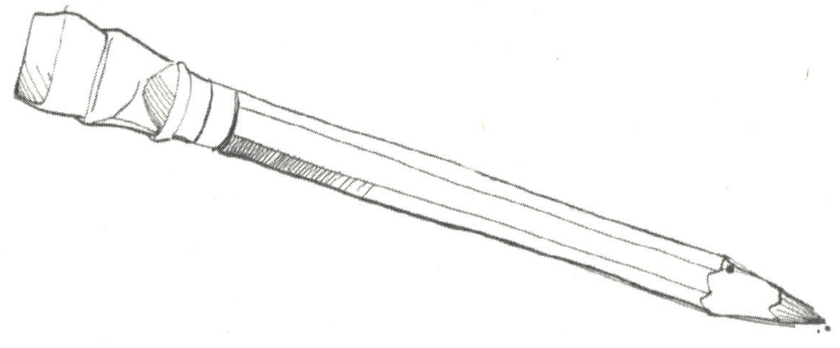

Can you be a great brand but a bad business proposition at the same time?

There is much talk today that the business is the brand and the brand is the business, but for me they are not exactly the same thing. Rather they are the yin and the yang of an organization – and the story of the Blackwing 602 pencil highlights that there is a difference.

Introduced by the Eberhard Faber Company during the Great Depression, the Blackwing 602 had a graphite-grey lacquer finish, a distinctive shape, an iconic foil-stamped logo, and an adjustable eraser housed in an extended ferrule. The pencils initially sold for 50 cents each.

Now, it wasn't what the pencil looked like that really made it different. It was what was on the inside and how that affected its performance. The Blackwing had an unusually smooth, soft-yet-durable lead, which allowed Faber to claim: "Half the Pressure, Twice the Speed."

The Blackwing 602 has a devoted following and a cult-like status. It has a list of celebrity endorsements any brand would be proud of, including Nobel-prize-winning authors, Oscar-winning animators and Grammy-winning songwriters.

"I have found a new kind of pencil–the best I have ever had. Of course, it costs three times as much, but it is black and soft but doesn't break off. I think I will always use these. They are called Blackwings and they really glide over the paper," said John Steinbeck, talking about his working habits in the *Paris Review.*

During a television interview with American talk-show host Charlie Rose, legendary animator Chuck Jones of Bugs Bunny and other Looney Tunes characters was asked about the "pen" he was using. Jones gently corrected him, then added: "A pen is full of ink. This [Blackwing] is full of ideas."

Despite this following of famous people and thousands of other users, the Blackwing was discontinued in 1998. The problem stemmed from one of those distinctive features – the extended eraser ferrule. It required special clips that were only produced on a custom-made machine. When Eberhard Faber was acquired and became part of Faber-Castell in 1994, they discovered that the machine was broken.

There were however sufficient clips that enabled production to continue until 1998. At this point, the company withdrew the Blackwing, claiming it was not commercially viable.

There was an immediate outcry and the pencils still in the supply chain were quickly bought-up and stockpiled. They began to appear on eBay and in the classified ads, and prices skyrocketed up to $55 for a single pencil.

Fans started looking for alternatives, and interest focused on Palomino's range of premium pencils, which many felt were comparable to the Blackwing. Palomino was soon being asked to consider reviving the iconic brand, the old unique look. Luckily Palomino founder and CEO Charles Berolzheimer, whose family's roots in the pencil industry dated back to the mid-19th century, was able to use his unique relationships to get permission to re-introduce the Blackwing pencil. Palomino introduced its new Blackwing in its original form (the 602) for true devotees, writers and everyday users, as well as a modified version with a slightly softer lead for artists. The new Palomino Blackwing 602 sold in packages of 12 for about $20.

And the moral of this story is that the brand is mightier than the business. What can you do to ensure you maintain your brand's equity in the face of business issues?

14. PROVOKING AN EMOTIONAL RESPONSE THE BIRDS EYE WAY

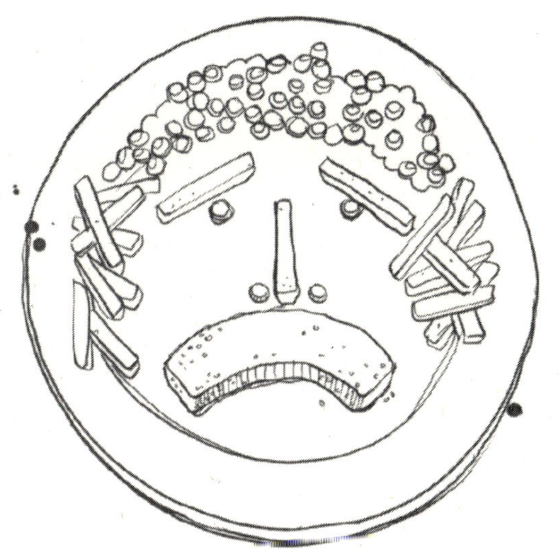

The best brands should appeal to more than your rational self: they should evoke an emotional response.

So, although it started with the Birds Eye beef burger, then went through an awkward phase over a ready meal, who would have thought the humble fish finger could end a romance?

In the 1970s, Mary's unrequited love for Ben, who only had eyes for his Birds Eye beef burgers, entertained the UK in one of the most famous British TV advertising campaigns of the time. (If you haven't seen them, enjoy https://www.youtube.com/watch?v=PGElZYKed88).

In the famous ad from the 1990s, Steve's friend Sean is distracted from his Birds Eye curry by Steve's mum who is getting ready to go out. Sean, slightly embarrassed, confesses: "I think I fancy your Mum." (Another 30 seconds well spent if you've never seen it before: https://www.youtube.com/watch?v=c4wAP8Xp63U).

Fast forward to 2013 and real life, fish fingers appear to have helped end scriptwriter Peter Morgan's marriage to Lila Schwarzenberg.

Peter Morgan, the scriptwriter behind films such as *The Queen*, *The Last King Of Scotland* and *Frost/Nixon*, married Lila Schwarzenberg – born Princess Anna Carolina zu Schwarzenberg – in 1997. The celebrity couple had five children and divided their time between Vienna and London.

Following their divorce, in a series of columns for a leading American magazine, Lila shed light on their tempestuous marriage and some of the moments that led to their parting.

"Peter . . . always says you can gauge the state of our marriage on the number of fish fingers he gets served up in a week," she wrote in 2013. "And it appears I went too far once again with my culinary neglect towards Peter as . . . I served him the leftovers of the kids' meal (guess what it was). He took one look and said: 'I am neither five years old nor a f***ing penguin.' He left the table and left the house in the search for a decent dinner."

And the moral is ...be careful what emotions you play with, you never know what might happen. What emotional responses do you want your brand to evoke?

15. THE INSIGHTFUL BASTARD

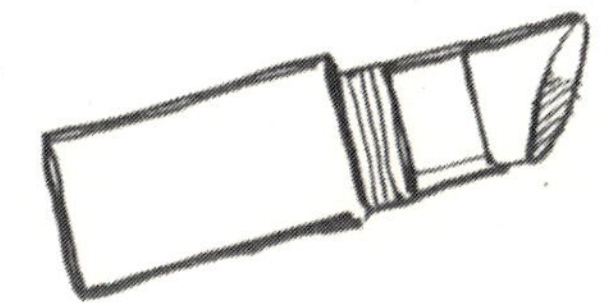

"Look, kiddie. I built this business by being a bastard. I run it by being a bastard. I'll always be a bastard, and don't you ever try to change me." So said Charles Haskell Revson to one of his senior colleagues.

Revson was known as a hard-working, hard-driven, highly competitive business executive who, on another occasion, said "I don't meet the competition, I destroy it".

He is perhaps most famous as the pioneering cosmetics industry executive who created and managed one of the world's leading cosmetic houses through five decades.

When Elka, the cosmetics company he had been working for, didn't promote him to the national distributor role he coveted, Revson decided to go into business for himself.

He teamed up with his brother, Joseph, and a chemist, Charles Lachman, and together they developed a unique manufacturing process that used pigments instead of dyes to create a new type of nail enamel in a variety of new attractive opaque colours. The story goes that Charles and Joseph were inspired by the scarlet-lipped, cigarette-smoking Hollywood actresses of the 1930s, believing what these women needed were red nails to match their red lips.

Lachman contributed his chemistry skills to the new company, as well as providing the 'l' for the new company's name – Revlon.

At first, Revlon's polishes were sold in beauty parlours with Revson as head salesman. Revson was known to put the nail polish on his own nails to demonstrate the colour, and he regularly criss-crossed the country by rail to promote it at every given opportunity.

In 1937, Revlon started selling in department stores and drug stores. But for Revson this was still just the beginning. By 1940, Revlon offered an entire manicure line, had added lipstick to the collection and, along the way, had become a multimillion-dollar organization. The expansion didn't stop there: Revlon went on to enter the perfume and fragrance market with great success.

Revson's drive to build the brand was never-ending and, in the mid-1950s, the company sponsored the quiz show The $64,000 Question, which was to become a television phenomenon and is said to have boosted sales considerably. However, the association wasn't without controversy. Revson and his brother Martin, second in charge at the company, allegedly demanded that the producers control the questions in order to keep contestants winning and maintain the programme's high ratings. This sparked what later became known as the quiz show scandal.

It is said that this, together with Charles' perfectionist nature, drove many of his former colleagues and partners out.

However, it is for another side of his nature that Charles is now remembered. He was an intuitive and insightful marketer, and the quote that is most often linked to his name is "in the factory we make cosmetics; in the drugstore we sell hope".

This highlights the difference between the functional nature of a product, and the emotional appeal of a brand.

And the moral is that there is a big difference between a product and a brand. What is it that you are really selling?

Footnote 1: It was a Revlon red nail enamel that Christian Louboutin apparently applied to the soles of one of his early designs. It was a huge success and, so obviously, became a permanent fixture. See Story 20, He Knows About Toes.

Footnote 2: Revson clearly wasn't just a hard-nosed businessman. In 1956, he established the Charles H Revson Foundation, which he funded with over $10 million during his lifetime. The foundation funded schools, hospitals, and service organizations serving the Jewish community, mostly located in New York. Upon his death, Revson endowed the foundation with $68 million from his estate, and granted the board of directors the discretion to chart the foundation's future course. In 1978, the foundation began a formal grant-making process, and since that time, it has disbursed a total of $145 million in grants, and its endowment has grown from $68 million to $141 million.

ORIGINS

Where did that brand come from?

When was it created?

Why was it created?

The origins of a brand is perhaps the richest source of a brand's tales because the reasons for its creation are so many and varied.

Many marketers will talk about how brands are created to answer customer needs, and indeed some are. Equally true is that some are down to men and women of vision, some are down to people who want to make a living, some are down to a particular problem that the brand owner faced, some borrow somebody else's idea, and some are down to pure luck and coincidence – the toss of a coin.

The circumstances in which an idea arrives are equally varied, and it is true to say that only in some of these stories were people actively looking to create a new brand.

16. THIRD TIME LUCKY

High profile, high margin and highly successful, but it was third time lucky for Nespresso.

It may be hard to believe now, but Nespresso was a failure not once but twice. It was only when Nestlé went outside its comfort zone and hired an outsider that a successful marketing mix was created.

The technology behind Nespresso was originally created in the Battelle Research Institute in Geneva, and the rights to it were acquired by Nestlé in 1974. In the following years the technology was refined and improved, and in 1982 the first version was launched. It was targeted at the restaurant trade in Switzerland as a means to allow smaller establishments to offer top quality coffee easily and economically, since it required no major capital investment and no need for specially trained staff. It failed to catch on, so it was back to the drawing board for Nestlé.

The second mix was to focus on the office coffee market. A deal was struck with a company who already operated in the office market to help ensure the new Nespresso System (the machines and the special coffee capsules) gained distribution. It was launched in Italy and then Japan in 1986. Unfortunately, it was way behind targets by mid-1987; only half of the manufactured machines had been sold, and capsule sales were poor too.

So in 1988 Nestlé did something different. It went outside to look for someone who could bring a new perspective, who wouldn't do things in the Nestlé way.

They hired Jean-Paul Gaillard, a young executive known for his flair and creativity, who had made his name at Philip Morris (the American global cigarette and tobacco company), having helped to transform its Marlboro Classics business.

Gaillard's actions were unexpected – his first strategic decision was to give up on the office business and focus on the household market. In other words, the man brought in to do something different wanted to take Nespresso into Nestlé's traditional market.

His second decision demonstrated his flair and creativity. Instead of selling through Nestlé's traditional channel – the grocery trade, Gaillard's plan was to split sales: selling the machines through department stores and other specialists; and the coffee capsules direct to owners. Instead of targeting Nestlé traditional mass market, he would position the brand as premium and exclusive. Gaillard's idea was to establish a Nespresso Club, which offered order taking around the clock, prompt delivery of fresh coffee (within two working days), and trained coffee specialists who could offer personalized advice and recommendations.

The initial research on this concept was poor and there was internal resistance from some Nestlé executives. Nevertheless, Gaillard and his team were so convinced that they were able to persuade the Nestlé CEO to let them continue. It has been said that one factor which helped sway the decision was Gaillard's obvious belief in his own idea. He offered to buy the rights for himself if Nestlé pulled the plug.

The club was launched in 1990 and was an immediate success.

And the moral is, sometimes approaching an existing market in a new way can be better than trying to play in a new market by existing rules. How could you bend the rules in your existing market?

Footnote: Jean-Paul Gaillard left the company in 1998, ten years after he joined. But he appears to have come back to haunt Nestlé, setting up a rival coffee-capsule company. The Ethical Coffee Company (ECC) aims to challenge Nestlé's dominance by selling cheaper, biodegradable pods that can be used in Nespresso machines. Nestlé has responded with legal proceedings against ECC – and another rival, Sara Lee – for alleged patent violations.

17. THE BILLION-DOLLAR BUTT

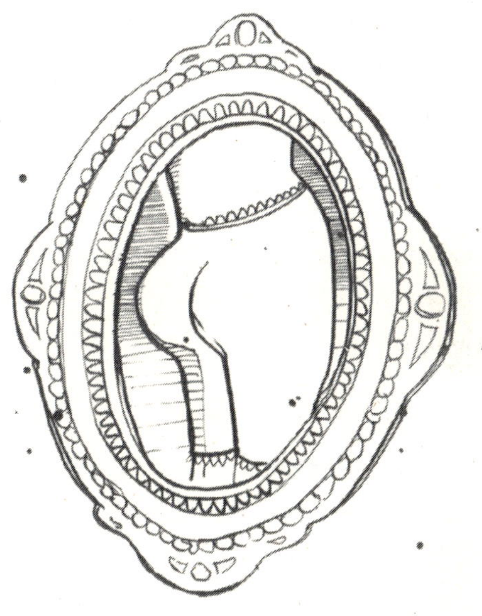

Sara Blakely believes she may be the only woman in the world that is actually grateful for cellulite and back fat.

That's because Blakely is the woman who turned an idea, and the $5,000 she had saved from selling fax machines, into a $250-million-a-year business.

And when asked where that idea came from, she was delightfully candid: "My inspiration was my own butt."

Working in the hot Florida climate, Blakeley disliked the appearance of a seamed foot with pantyhose, especially when she wore open-toed shoes. But she liked the fact that the control-top of the pantyhose eliminated panty lines and made her body, and her butt, appear firmer.

When cutting the bottom off normal pantyhose didn't work (the cut-off material on the legs rolled up too much), she started a search to find the right material. Eventually coming upon a solution in a craft store, she wrote her own patent following instructions from a Barnes & Noble textbook, and incorporated her company under the name Spanx.

Not only candid, she is clearly committed to her cause. Once she had had her first samples made, she looked up companies in the Yellow Pages to find potential stockists. Having identified Neiman Marcus as exactly the sort of store she wanted to sell Spanx, she set off to convince the buyer of the merits of her new pants.

Blakely believes in the power of a product demonstration, and it wasn't long before she was in the restroom showing off her inspirational butt, demonstrating what it looked like before and after putting on Spanx.

It was a demonstration that got Spanx its first listing, in seven Neiman Marcus stores.

When Blakely told the Spanx sample manufacturer about the Neiman Marcus deal, his response wasn't quite the one she had been expecting. He clearly wasn't as convinced of the likely appeal of Spanx. Blakely recalls him saying: "I thought these were just going to be Christmas gifts for the next five years."

Blakely however was determined that Spanx was going to be a success, and she wasn't going to leave anything to chance. She started to call up everyone she knew who lived near those first Neiman Marcus stores and asked them to buy a pair of Spanx, promising that she'd reimburse their money.

"Right when I was running out of friends and money," Blakely and Spanx got their lucky break... "Oprah named them as one of her favourite things," she says.

That changed everything. Distribution spread quickly to Bloomingdales, Saks and Bergdorf Goodman. In 2001, she signed a contract with QVC, the home shopping channel, where she sold 8,000 pairs in the first six minutes.

Blakely is now the world's youngest female self-made billionaire, according to *Forbes* magazine. And you could say Blakely is the lady with the first billion-dollar butt.

And the moral is, it pays to truly believe in your brand. How far are you willing to go to help your brand succeed?

18. THE ALLIGATOR BAG AND THE POLO SHIRT

Frenchman René Lacoste was a tennis player, a very good tennis player. He won seven grand slam titles, and was for two consecutive years in the late 1920s ranked as number one in the world.

He wasn't, however, a fan of the tennis clothes of the time. He found traditional 'tennis whites', which comprised long-sleeved button-down shirts, long trousers and a tie, very restrictive. It was a lot of clothing to be wearing when racing to the net to reach for a drop shot, or when stretching up for an overhead smash.

In a 1979 article in *People* magazine, he remembered how he found a solution: "One day I noticed my friend the

Marquis of Cholmondeley, wearing his polo shirt on the court, 'A practical idea,' I thought to myself."

It was so practical, in fact, that René commissioned an English tailor to whip up a few shirts in both cotton and wool for him. And it was at the US Open in New York City in 1926 that Lacoste made his first appearance in his new shirt. "Soon everyone was wearing them," he recalled.

Coincidentally, it was around that same time Lacoste acquired his nickname – crocodile.

While there is no debate over the nickname itself, there is still some debate as to why and how he acquired that particular name. The least polite, and indeed the least favoured, was that it was a reference to his slightly long and pointy nose. Others say the name came from his athletic dynamism and boldness.

However, the most oft-quoted reason is that it was the result of a bet with the captain of the French Davis Cup, who wagered him an alligator suitcase on the result of his 1927 match.

Unfortunately, René lost the match and went back to France empty-handed, but with the tale of the "alligator" preceeding him. "Alligator" somehow became "crocodile" when he was back in France.

Whatever the source, Lacoste embraced his new moniker. And when his friend, Robert George, sketched a crocodile for him, he immediately had it embroidered onto all of his shirts. It became his personal brand… before he even had the product to go with it.

That, however, was to change once he retired from tennis in the early 1930s. He set up a company called La Chemise Lacoste in 1933 with another friend, André Gillier, who had been president of the largest French knitwear company at the time, and they started to produce and sell crocodile-emblazoned shirts.

Lacoste is still making and selling shirts with the distinctive green crocodile. Though today they are worn for much more than just tennis.

And the moral is that the best brands create distinctive personalities. How are you nurturing your brand's personality?

19. HOW BEN AND JERRY BUILT THEIR BRAND ON A $5 CORRESPONDENCE COURSE, A SOCIAL CONSCIENCE AND A SENSE OF HUMOUR

What is the recipe for success if you want to create one of the world's most famous food brands?

Well, if that brand is Ben and Jerry's you need two friends, a $5 correspondence course, a social conscience, a sense of humour and …an ability to turn a problem into an opportunity.

Ben Cohen and Jerry Greenfield were childhood friends from New York. Jerry went to college, but afterwards found himself unable to make his way into medical school. Ben, too, had started college, but soon dropped out. He tried his hand at becoming a potter, but without much success.

So, in 1977, the two friends sent off for, and completed, a $5 correspondence course on ice-cream making, which they purchased from Pennsylvania State University's Creamery.

It was during this period that the pair discovered a problem: Ben suffered from anosmia – the inability to perceive odour. A sense of smell is normally a key requirement for any budding chef, and this could potentially have held the boys back. Instead, Ben started developing recipes relying more on taste rather than aroma. This led to the brand's adoption of its trademark chunky pieces which became the source for many of its tongue-in-cheek names like Chubby Hubby, Chunky Monkey, Karamel Sutra and Cherry Garcia.

The next problem was where to open their first premises. "Our dream was to open an ice cream store in a nice warm college town. But all of those towns already had ice cream stores, so we ended up in Burlington, Vermont."

Using a $12,000 investment, $4,000 of which they had to borrow, the two business partners duly opened their ice cream parlour in a renovated gas station on 5 May 1978.

Right from the start, Ben and Jerry were committed to doing good.

"From the very beginning, before we were even profitable, we always gave back. We sponsored events, like free ice cream day, outdoor movies and street festivals. Our business was ice cream, but our real mission was building community, making a difference, and having fun. Maybe that's why our customers stuck with us through those long, cold

Vermont winters. Two years later, when we started making money, it was only natural to support our loyal community with grants."

In 1979, they marked their anniversary by holding the first-ever free-cone day, now an international annual celebration.

In 1980, they rented space in an old spool-and-bobbin mill on South Champlain Street in Burlington, and began packing their ice cream in pints. These were distributed to grocery and 'mom-and-pop' stores along the restaurant-delivery routes that Ben had been servicing out of the back of his old VW Squareback wagon.

In 1981, the first Ben & Jerry's franchise store opened on Route 7 in Shelburne, Vermont. In 1982 the old gas station was demolished to create a parking lot. Just before the wrecking ball was swung, the new Ben & Jerry's on Cherry Street in Burlington was up & scooping.

In 1985, The Ben & Jerry's Foundation was established, with a gift from Ben and Jerry – 7.5% of the company's annual pre-tax profits was donated to fund community-oriented projects.

The creation of the foundation also formalized the concept of the "Double Dip – running a values-led business and making money too". It became the title for their 1998 best-selling book and, in the same year, the two men were announced as US Small Business Persons of the year, an honour that was awarded by the then US President Ronald Reagan.

And the moral is that the best brands give something back to their communities. What should your brand be giving back?

20. HE KNOWS ABOUT TOES

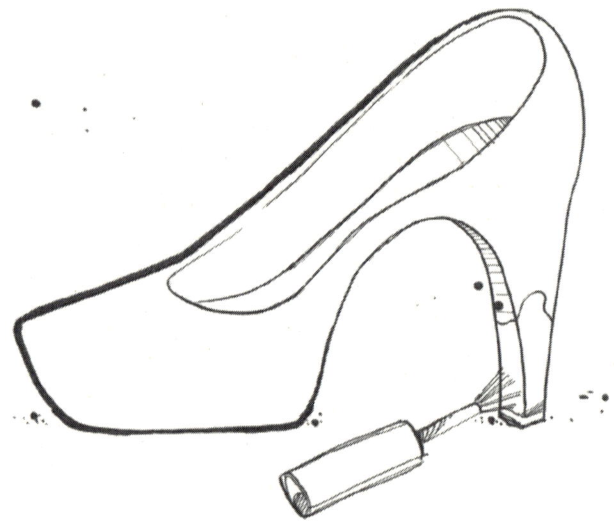

In his own words, Christian Louboutin "knows about toes", so it's not surprising that he wanted nail polish to be his first foray into the beauty world.

In September 2014, the world-famous shoe designer launched a range of 31 nail varnishes. This was a move which in many ways represented the repayment of an old debt, as the initial success of the Christian Louboutin shoe brand owes much to a bottle of nail varnish.

Louboutin was born in Paris in 1963. When he was 12, a museum next door to the family's apartment had a poster outside with a sketch of a stiletto on it. Christian became obsessed with the poster, he sketched and resketched it and soon realized that he wanted to be a shoe designer.

He started missing school. "I was out every night. I have a piece of paper which says that I missed 92 days in one year." He spent his time with friends, partying and watching the showgirls from The Folies Bergère and the Moulin Rouge, whose costumes and shoes fascinated him.

At 18 he got a job at Charles Jourdan. He went on to do freelance work for Chanel and Yves Saint Laurent, then went to work in leather factories in Naples and Florence. He returned to Paris and went to work for Roger Vivier, a man he credits with teaching him much of what he knows.

Upset when Vivier died, Christian decided on a change of direction, and became a landscape gardener. However he was soon missing shoes, and started to spend hours drawing them and creating his own designs.

Then shortly after the death of his mother, and at the urging of an antique dealer friend, he decided to go back to his first love, shoes.

"He said just go for it. That same week, I had dinner with my two oldest friends, Henri and Bruno, and they said yeah, let's do it. They say don't mix business with pleasure, but 23 years on we're even better friends than before. Henri married my sister, and Bruno is the president of the company."

However, despite all the drawing and designs he had done over the years, when he saw his new prototype he had a feeling something still wasn't quite right.

"My drawing of it was better, I couldn't understand what it was. Then I turned it over and realized that the percentage of black was huge, but there was no black in my drawing. My assistant was painting her nails, so I grabbed her nail polish, painted the sole and it popped. It gave definition to the heel. It illuminated the shoe."

His new scarlet-soled shoes were an immediate success, and Louboutin is now a global brand with stores in over 50 countries.

Now the brand is planning a new move, and soon you will be able to paint your nails the same colour as your heels with a bottle of Rouge Louboutin.

Each 16-faceted glass bottle has an 8-inch stiletto-like cap featuring a red underside, just like its muse. The spiky lid is the same height as the Ballerina Ultima, which is the brand's tallest shoe, so you can not only match your bag and shoes but match your nails too.

"The red sole was born from red nail polish. I am giving back to nails what the shoes took from the nails many years ago."

And the moral is that it pays to make your brand truly distinctive. How do you ensure distinctiveness in your brand?

21. JOHAN'S 'SATIABLE CURIOSITY'

In *The Elephant's Child*, Rudyard Kipling writes: "The great grey-green, greasy Limpopo River, all set about with fever-trees." However this is not only the place to which the elephant's child took "his satiable curtiosity" and ended up with his "blackish, bulgy nose" stretched into a trunk, it is where Peppadew, the brand of sweet piquanté peppers was discovered and is now grown.

The story of the first new fruit to be introduced to the world market since the arrival of the kiwi, begins near the Limpopo river, South Africa, one day in 1993. Businessman and farmer Johan Steenkamp was looking around the garden of his holiday home in the Eastern Cape in South Africa when he spotted an unusual-looking bush. It stood head high and was laden with small bright red fruit, which to Johan looked like a cross between a miniature red pepper and a cherry tomato.

Johan obviously had some of the elephant's child's "satiable curtiosity" so gingerly bit into one. He was rewarded with a unique, delicious peppery, yet sweet, taste.

Johan was later to discover that the plant was a cultivar (a type of plant selected for its specific characteristics and maintained that way by propagation) of the Capsicum baccatum. He also found out that they have a mild heat of around 1,177 on the Scoville scale (which measures the spicy heat of peppers), but he never discovered where his bush originated from.

"Where the plant is native to is still open to debate, but we think it's from Central America. I also have my suspicions about how it came to South Africa, because the previous owner of the house where Johan first discovered it was a botanist who had travelled quite extensively in Central America," said Phil Ovens, now managing director of Peppadew International.

Realizing he might have hit upon something really new, Johan saved some seeds from that first crop which he then cultivated. In the meantime, he developed a secret pickling recipe that is still used today. Johan then began bottling and selling his peppers locally.

He christened his new brand Peppadew – a portmanteaux name blending the fruit's peppery taste with the fresh, light imagery of the morning dew.

Had he done so a few thousand years earlier, the elephant's child could have added a few hundred jars of Peppadew to the provisions he took on his fateful journey to the Limpopo River – the "hundred pounds of bananas (the little short red kind), and a hundred pounds of sugar-cane (the long purple kind), and seventeen melons (the greeny-crackly kind)".

And the moral is, sometimes a good idea is sitting right in front of you. What is so obvious that you might have missed it?

22. THE OPTOMETRIST AND THE NATIONALIST

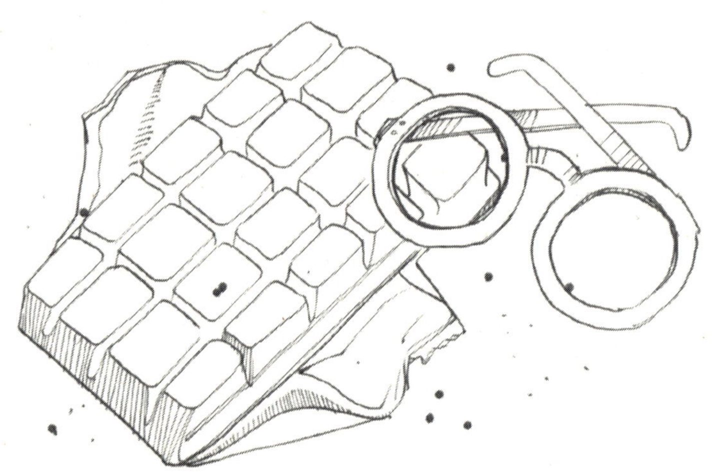

Fazer Blue, or more specifically *Fazerin Sininen* in Finnish, is a truly iconic chocolate brand in Finland, where it is sometimes described as part of the cultural heritage.

First launched in 1922, it still regularly tops the annual brand study by the local *Markkinointi & Mainonta* [Marketing & Advertising] magazine.

Though it bears the name of the company founder Karl Fazer on its distinctive blue wrapper, its origins owe as much to his son Sven.

Karl Otto Fazer was born in Helsinki in 1866, and against his father's wishes, decided to become a confectioner. He had studied baking in Berlin, Paris and Saint Petersburg before opening a French-Russian confectionery at Glogatan 3 in Helsinki on 17 September 1891. Its success allowed him to go on to open a chocolate factory in Rödbergen.

Sven joined the now-thriving business with his father's blessing, and it was Sven who came across the recipe that was to become Fazer Blue.

Sven was working in the factory with an English machine supplier called Shaller, and one day discovered that Shaller's son-in-law was suffering from an eye disease.

As it happened, one of Sven's relatives was an optometrist, to whom Sven kindly introduced Shaller. The doctor was able to cure Shaller's son-in-law's problem, but refused to take any payment for his work.

Feeling that he needed to give something back to the family, Shaller presented Sven with a special recipe for milk chocolate, which he had received from a Swiss master confectioner.

It was this recipe that was the foundation for Fazer Blue.

It was Karl, however, who chose to put the new chocolate in its blue wrapper. Now, blue is a colour of particular significance to Finnish people, evoking feelings of peace, nature and national pride.

Another Finnish concept that may have been in Karl's mind was '*sininen hetki*', a 'blue moment' – the specific time, usually near dawn or dusk, when the landscape is tinged with blue. It is a moment strongly associated with peace and tranquillity. Indeed, some years later Fazer was to use the notion of "*sininen hetki*" in its advertising, suggesting Fazer Blue was the chocolate "for little blue moments".

A number of writers believe, however, that the real reason Karl chose blue was because he was a nationalist. Blue had long been one of Finland's 'national' colours. The country's flag is blue and white.

Finland had only declared its independence in 1917; it had previously been the Russian Grand Duchy of Finland. Karl, like many others, objected to the 'Russification' of Finland in the two decades leading up to it.

Examples of this Russification, include when the Russian-dominated government forbid the use of Finnish stamps and abolished the Finnish mail service, replacing it with a Russian system. As an act of defiance, Karl printed Finnish stamps on his chocolate wrappers, along with pictures of important Finnish men.

Blue was therefore the obvious choice for a true natioalist like Karl. The choice of the particular shade of Fazer blue was to become particularly important. Fazer was the first company in Finland to patent a colour. The trademark blue was patented on 30 April 2001, meaning that only Fazer is allowed to sell or advertise products with that specific shade.

Funnily enough, while it is almost universally referred to as Fazer Blue, the word "blue" isn't and never has been used on the packaging. The company's website notes that: "Indeed, the colour is a symbol of the product and the word "blue" does not even need to be mentioned."

And the moral is that the visual clues can be stronger than written ones. What could you say better in images and colours about your brand?

23. THE COLONEL, THE SECRET RECIPE AND THE 600 HANDSHAKES

What do Fred Astaire, Whoopi Goldberg, Elvis Presley, Pope John Paul II and Colonel Harland Sanders have in common?

They were all, in fact, Kentucky Colonels. A Kentucky Colonel is not a military title. It is the highest title of honour that can be bestowed by the Commonwealth of Kentucky. Commissions are given by the Governor and the Secretary of State to individuals in recognition of noteworthy accomplishments and outstanding service to a community, state or the nation – and Harland Sanders was commissioned twice.

Harland Sanders was born in 1890 and raised on a farm outside Henryville, Indiana. When he was six, his father died and his mother was forced to go to work, so young Harlan was left to take care of his three-year-old sibling. This meant he had to do much of the family cooking and, by the time he was seven, he had mastered a range of dishes.

Leaving home at 13, Sanders didn't immediately put these cooking skills into practice. Instead he held a series of jobs, including farm hand, streetcar conductor, army private in Cuba, blacksmith's assistant, rail yard fireman, insurance salesman and tyre salesman.

In 1930, at the age of 40, his career took another turn and he took over a Shell filling station on US Route 25, just outside North Corbin, a small city on the edge of the Appalachian Mountains in Kentucky.

He quickly converted a storeroom into a small eating area, using his own dining table, and started serving meals to hungry travellers. He multi-tasked as a station operator, chief cook and cashier.

He prospered and, in 1934, Sanders purchased the larger filling station on the other side of the road, expanded to six tables, and began to sell fried chicken. For the next several years he experimented with recipes, trying to find the perfect recipe for his chicken. He finally settled on what is now known as The Original Recipe – a secret blend of 11 herbs and spices. Although he never publicly revealed the recipe, he admitted to the use of salt and pepper, and claimed that the ingredients "stand on everybody's shelf".

In the meantime, and to improve his skills, Sanders took an eight-week restaurant management course at the Cornell University School of Hotel Administration.

By 1936 his business had proved so successful that he was given his first title of Kentucky Colonel by Governor Ruby Laffoon. In the following year, Sanders expanded his restaurant to 140 seats. In 1940 he purchased a motel across the street and named it The Sanders Court & Café.

It was only after being re-commissioned as a Kentucky Colonel in 1950, this time by Governor Lawrence Wetherby, that Sanders began to dress the part (he grew a goatee beard and started wearing a black frock coat, which he later switched to a white suit with a string tie), and started referring to himself as Colonel. His associates and employees went along with the title change, "jokingly at first and then in earnest", according to his biographer, Josh Ozersky.

Then, in 1955, his fortunes changed: an interstate highway was built to bypass Corbin, redirecting most of the passing traffic away from his restaurant and motel.

Sanders sold up.

Showing true entrepreneurial spirit, the Colonel decided to see if he could develop a different business model based on his increasingly famous chicken. He would develop a franchise operation. Sanders started travelling across the country by car, cooking his chicken for restaurant owners and their employees. If the reaction was favourable, Sanders offered them a deal – sealed with a handshake – which stipulated a nickel payment for each chicken the restaurant sold.

This wasn't a completely new idea. In 1952, Sanders successfully franchised his chicken recipe to Pete Harman, the operator of one of the largest restaurants in Salt Lake City.

Harman was to play a big part in the success of the new operation, though, and has been described as the "virtual co-founder" of the chain.

It was Harman who hired Don Anderson, a sign painter who coined the phrase "Kentucky fried chicken". Sanders adopted the name because it distinguished his product from the deep-fried "Southern fried chicken" product found in other restaurants. Harman claimed in his first year of selling "Kentucky fried chicken", his restaurant sales more than tripled.

It was Harman who trademarked the phrase "It's finger lickin' good", and in 1957 it was Harman who came up with the original 'bucket' offer. He conceived the idea as a favour to Sanders, who had called on behalf of a Denver franchisee who had bought 500 cardboard buckets from a travelling salesman and had no idea what to do with them. Harman suggested "bundling" 14 pieces of chicken, five bread rolls and a pint of gravy into a cardboard bucket, and offered it to families as "a complete meal" for US$3.50 (around US$30 in 2014!).

By 1964 there were 600 franchise outlets across the United States and Canada, and, deciding to call time on his career, Colonel Sanders sold his interest in the United States operations for $2 million.

Colonel Harland Sanders passed away on 16 December 1980, aged 90.

And the moral is that the best brands can be built on a variety of business systems. Is there a new business model that could transform your brand?

24. HEADS OR TAILS

"Heads, and we'll start a casserole café; Tails, and it'll be the beauty boutique." Jean and Jane Ford's future rested on the toss of a coin.

After graduating from Indiana University, Jean and Jane, six-foot-tall identical twins, moved to New York to try and break into the modelling world. While they got some I. Magnin and Macy's catalogue work, they had to supplement this with sales clerking and cleaning jobs.

So, in 1973, they decided to move to San Francisco. "I came to find a husband," Jane has later admitted, while Jean felt she needed to move before she was shoved! "I came because I'd burned every bridge with my partying."

A year later they got what was to be their most famous modelling assignment – as the girls in the Calgon Bath Bead commercials. "They'd wanted blond twins," the distinctly brunette Jean says, "and couldn't find any that could talk. So they showed us a script and said, 'They can speak! Sign them up!' It was a major gas."

A couple of years later, and after receiving a stern "don't waste your education" letter from their mother, they decided they'd better try and put that education to good use. After much discussion, it came down to two ideas. Unable to make up their minds they agreed to leave the final choice to chance – the toss of a coin: heads, they'd open a casserole café; tails, a cosmetics store.

Tails it was, and in 1976 the sisters opened "the Face Place" in San Francisco's Mission District.

The transition from beauty place to cosmetics brand started soon after with an unusual request from an unusual customer.

Jean picks up the story…

"One morning, a worn-out stripper walked into the store. Her shirt, some tie-dyed thing. The fishnets broken up. She was wasted. She put both arms on the counter, and she said, "Hiii". Drunk. She said, "I need somethin' special." That something special was in fact something to keep her nipples pink. Apparently, whatever she was applying was wearing off mid-performance because, "when I dance, I sweat".

So Jane and I looked at each other and said: "We have that. It's just not here right now. Come back tomorrow. Jane came over to my apartment, and we got a bunch of red food colouring, glycerine, rose petals...and we put it in the blender and boiled it down to a reduction. It was so strong!"

They poured some into two little glass vials that had corks in them. Jane drew a rose and added the words "rose tint", and they glued it onto the bottles.

Jane recalls: "The gal comes in the next day–same outfit–to get her goods. She came back a week later and said, 'I've run out, and all my friends want it.' She said, "My tribe needs this." We said, "Friday we'll have 24 more bottles for your weekend.'"

From there demand took off, and as Jean remembers, it was initially a very targeted crowd. "Strippers, ballerinas, gay guys, all coming in: 'I want that Rose Tint.'" But soon it began selling to a much wider audience. It was renamed Benetint in 1990, and is now marketed as a lip and cheek stain. It is still the brand's best-seller, with over 10 million bottles sold to a clientele that now includes Sarah Jessica Parker, Nicole Kidman, Kate Hudson, and romance novelist Danielle Steel.

The brand was also renamed in 1990, and is now known globally as benefit – and it lives by the girls' own quirky philosophy:

The Benefesto

We believe in whistling while you work it
And faking it 'til you make it

We believe in fast & fabulous beauty solutions
And that glamour is grabbing life by the giggles
And not letting go

We believe if at first you don't succeed, apply more lipstick
That sexy gets you everywhere
And if you can't be good be gorgeous

We believe laughter is the best cosmetic!

And the moral is, every brand needs a little luck... but you need to use it when you get it. Have you recently had a piece of good fortune and have you exploited it?

25. A MAN OF VISION, PERSEVERANCE AND CURIOSITY

Clarence Birdseye was a man of vision, perseverance and, above all, curiosity. By the time he died, on 7 October 1956, he held roughly 300 patents including ones for incandescent lighting, a harpoon for marking whales, an infrared heating process, a process for dehydrating food, and a technique for converting sugar cane waste into paper pulp. He wrote a book on wildflowers, and was an expert at Chinese checkers.

He once said: "I have more hobbies than the law allows. Some are sissy. Some have hairs on their chest."

However, he is best known for something completely different – US Patent #1,773,079; a double belt fast freezing machine. This invention gave birth to today's frozen food industry and the brand that still bears his name.

Clarence Birdseye was born in New York, in 1886. He was the sixth of nineteen children! Interested in zoology and botany, he enrolled as a student at Amherst College but dropped out before the end of the course due to financial difficulties.

He began a career as a taxidermist, but his curiosity drove him to try his hand as an assistant naturalist, and he later worked with entomologist Willard Van Orsdel King. Clarence's role was to capture several hundred small mammals from which King removed several thousand ticks. King used them in his research to identify ticks as the cause of Rocky Mountain spotted fever.

Deciding he wanted a new challenge, Birdseye accepted a field assignment in Labrador in the Dominion of Newfoundland (now part of Canada).

It was here that he noticed the local Inuit tribespeople would freeze the fish they caught under very thick layers of ice. This, combined with the -40°C weather, meant the fish froze almost instantly but, more importantly, when the fish was thawed out and cooked, it tasted fresh and delicious.

He immediately recognized the potential, as the quality was far higher than the frozen seafood sold in New York.

In 1922, having conducted fish-freezing experiments at the Clothel Refrigerating Company, he started using chilled air (at -43°C) to freeze fish fillets. He then established his own company, Birdseye Seafoods Inc, but in 1924 the company went bankrupt due to lack of demand.

He refused to give up, and later that same year developed an entirely new process which involved packing fish into cartons, then freezing them between two refrigerated surfaces – all done under pressure. Birdseye created a new company, the General Seafood Corporation, to promote this method.

In 1925, the General Seafood Corporation moved to Gloucester, Massachusetts. There it employed Birdseye's new method – the "double belt freezer", in which cold brine chilled a pair of stainless steel belts carrying packaged fish, freezing the fish even more quickly. It became US Patent #1,773,079.

This quick-freeze method produced even better results, and by 1927 Birdseye extended the process to meat, poultry, fruit and vegetables.

In 1929, Birdseye sold his company and accompanying patents for $22 million to Goldman Sachs and the Postum Company, which eventually became General Foods Corporation, and which in turn founded the Birds Eye Frozen Food Company.

Clarence continued to work with the company as a consultant, further developing frozen food technology, but now he also had the time and money to indulge his curiosity in all his other hobbies.

And the moral is, great brands can be built on vision, curiosity and perseverance. Have you got these three qualities in your brand team?

26. MURDER MOST PROFITABLE

Anthony E Pratt was a small-time but reasonably successful musician, who during the inter-war period earned his living playing the piano in country hotels and on cruise ships.

He was a lover of detective fiction, and his favourite authors were Raymond Chandler and Agatha Christie. It was perhaps not surprising that he also enjoyed the regular murder mystery evenings held at the country hotels where he played.

These mysteries would involve hotel guests and a few actors playing characters in a plot that revolved around the murder of one or more of the other guests. Most of the hotels had many rooms giving them the scope and space for the mystery to unfold and, ultimately, solved as different clues were found.

When World War II started, Pratt took a job in an engineering factory in Birmingham that manufactured components for tanks. Working on a drilling machine, he found the work rather tedious but it did give him time to think. He was later to describe himself as "an introvert full of ruminations, speculations and imaginative notions".

One of those imaginative notions led to him to develop a murder-mystery-themed board game, which he originally and somewhat unimaginatively named "Murder!" The artwork was designed by his wife Elva. And on 12 January 1944, he filed a provisional specification at the UK Patent Office.

Later that year, the Pratts visited Waddington's Games in Leeds, England, to discuss the possibilities for its manufacture. Waddington's managing director Norman Watson played a game and immediately snapped it up.

However, due to war-time shortages of various materials, the game's launch was delayed. It finally went on sale in 1949, by which time a licensing deal with Parker Brothers in the United States had also been struck.

Pratt's original game featured ten characters. These ten included the later eliminated Mr. Brown, Mr. Gold, Miss Grey, and Mrs. Silver, along with two who were re-named Nurse White, and Colonel Yellow. There had been eleven rooms on the original board designed by Elva but the gun room and cellar were dropped. There were many weapons. Not all made the new cut.

Its name also changed, twice. Norman Watson suggested Cluedo (a combination of 'clue', and 'ludo' – Latin for I play) as an alternative to 'Murder', and Parker Brothers shortened this to 'Clue' for the US market.

Cluedo, or Clue, is today sold in over 40 countries, from Brazil to Sweden, New Zealand to Abu Dhabi. In Brazil the game has acquired a third name, 'Detective'. So while it is clear that people all over the world love a good murder mystery game, you, dear reader, are among the few who, when it comes to its inventor, know whodunnit.

And the moral is, brands can be built on 'imaginative notions'. Where will your brand find some new 'imaginative notions'?

27. A FASHION FAIRYTALE, A MARKETING MASTERCLASS

The Diane von Fürstenberg story is a fashion fairytale and an interesting lesson in branding.

The fashion narrative runs something like this: a beautiful, free-spirited, young, European princess arrives in New York in the early 1970s and makes her fortune, is pictured on the cover of *Newsweek* before she is 30, but then loses her way in business. She moves to Paris, gets divorced, remarries thereby losing her title. Then in her 50s she stages a comeback and runs a business that is more successful than ever, with 85 stores worldwide.

The lesson in branding begins in her childhood. She once told Oprah Winfrey that, as a little girl, "I didn't know what I wanted to do, but I knew the kind of woman I wanted to be – an independent woman, who drives her own cars and pays her own bills".

Then in 1970, with a $30,000 investment, she began designing women's clothes. "The minute I knew I was about to be Egon's (that's Prince Egon of Fürstenberg's) wife, I decided to have a career. I wanted to be someone of my own, and not just a plain little girl who got married beyond her desserts."

Shortly afterwards, she met with then *Vogue* editor Diana Vreeland, who declared her designs "absolutely smashing" and had her name listed on the Fashion Calendar for New York Fashion Week – a vital stepping stone in building her brand.

However, at the core of her story is a dress.

A jersey wrap dress, made without buttons or zips, dubbed "The Most Empowering Dress Ever" by *Marie Claire* in 2014, 40 years after its launch.

Fürstenberg's design came from observation, not formal market research, as she explained in her 1998 autobiography, *Diane, A Signature Life*. "I had no focus groups, no marketing surveys, no plan. All I had was an instinct that women wanted a fashion option besides hippie clothes, bell-bottoms and stiff pantsuits that hid their femininity… The dresses made sense. They were sexy and practical. There were very few businesswomen at the time, and the few in management tended to play down their gender by dressing more like men than like women.

"It allowed women to go to work and still feel like a woman. I scribbled a little something on a white cube in one of my first ads and it is still true today: 'Feel like a woman, wear a dress.' Your most authentic self is always your most powerful self."

The choice of material for the dress was a very conscious one. Asked to explain it she noted that it is female designers – "Coco Chanel, Donna Karan, me" – who dress women in jersey, "because we know it feels great and lets you get on with your day, and we care about that".

When asked about its undeniable sex appeal, she famously replied: "Well, if you're trying to slip out without waking a sleeping man, zips are a nightmare."

It was, and indeed still is, a dress for women who choose clothes for freedom, movement and self-determination. "That's what my brand does," she says. "We sell confidence."

And that confidence comes from a combination of comfort and glamour.

The concept of a wrap design was nothing new; it's a technique which probably predates sewing and is worn by women in many parts of the world. Dior translated the idea into high fashion in the 1960s. But what made the von Fürstenberg dress was its cut, its cloth and its neckline: it was pretty, practical and, if required, provocative.

Within two years she'd sold five million dresses and was featured on the cover of *Newsweek*. The cover was intended to be Gerald Ford, who had just won his first Republican Presidential Primary, but this was changed last minute. The accompanying article declared her "the most marketable woman since Coco Chanel".

Talking to *The Guardian* newspaper recently, she admitted that she often "took that dress for granted, even though it paid my bills, paid for my children's education, my apartment on Fifth Avenue and my house in the country. To be honest, sometimes I even resented it. But now, finally, I see: this dress is actually bigger than me. I am just a conduit for the dress... It is so much the essence of my brand. I became who I am because of that dress, because the dress is everything my brand stands for".

And the moral is, brands can be built on consumer understanding. How well do you understand the lives and motivations of your consumer?

28. ALL WRAPPED UP

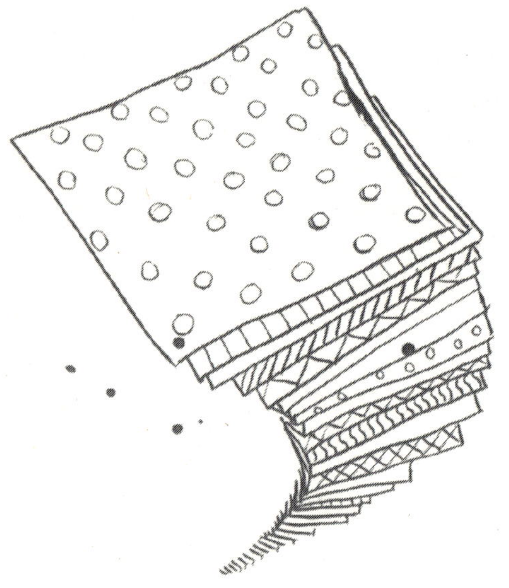

Japanese furoshiki, the reusable wrapping cloth still in use today, has been around since the Edo period (1603 – 1868). The similar Korean wrapping cloth, bojagi, dates back to the Three Kingdoms Period, possibly as early as the first century AD.

In the West, using paper as a covering for gifts has a shorter history, and one skewed to the wealthier end of society.

Upper-class Victorians regularly used heavy, elaborately decorated paper, topped with ribbons and lace to wrap and conceal gifts, especially at Christmas. The less wealthy parts of Victorian society couldn't afford the paper, but that didn't really matter much since their limited resources often didn't even stretch to presents.

By the early 20th century, Christmas and other gifting occasions had increased, and the thick, unwieldy paper used by the Victorians had given way to cheaper and easier-to-use plain tissue paper, most often red, green, or white.

In 1917, however, necessity was to be the mother of invention, and wrapping paper was changed irrevocably.

Brothers Joyce (JC) and Rollie were running a stationery store in Kansas City, Missouri. Business was good in the run up to Christmas – so good, in fact, that they ran out of their standard tissue paper.

They decided that they couldn't rely on their father's, an itinerant preacher, maxim "the Lord will provide", but should follow JC's mantra instead. His belief was that "it's a good idea to give the Lord a little help".

Searching through what they had, they came across a stack of "fancy French paper". Paper meant not for display, but for lining envelopes. They decided to put it on sale and price it at $0.10 a sheet. They quickly sold reams.

As JC was to say later: "The decorative gift-wrapping business was born on the day Rollie placed those French envelope linings on top of that showcase."

During the holiday season of 1918, the brothers decided to see if their idea was more than a one-year wonder, and again offered the lining papers as gift wrap, this time priced at $0.25 for three sheets. Again, the sheets sold out.

So in 1919, confident that there was a market, the brothers began producing and selling their own printed decorative papers, designed for the sole purpose of wrapping gifts.

The brothers' name was Hall, their brand was Hallmark, and for years they had the gift-paper market all wrapped up.

And the moral is that sometimes necessity can be the mother of invention. What opportunities can you find in any moments of adversity you face?

29. SALESMANSHIP DOWN TO A TEA

Phineas Taylor "PT" Barnum is often considered to be the world's greatest showman. However, another 19th century entrepreneur who used a number of the same techniques, and is still known around the world, was Thomas J Lipton.

Lipton was born in Glasgow, Scotland, in 1850, and at the age of 15 travelled to the United States. There he worked on a Virginia tobacco farm, a rice plantation in South Carolina, a streetcar in New Orleans, before finding a job in a department store's grocery section in New York City. It was here he witnessed "American" merchandising in action and learnt the lessons he would employ so successfully later in life.

Unlike millions of others who had left for the United States never to return, Lipton saved up his earnings and went back to Scotland. After briefly working in the family grocery store, he opened his own in 1871 at 101 Stobcross Street in the Anderston area of Glasgow.

To announce the launch, he organized a headline-grabbing parade of what he called the "largest hogs in captivity", each of which carried a sign proclaiming: "I'm going to Lipton's. The best shop in town for Irish bacon!"

Other publicity-generating stunts included importing the world's largest cheese, and issuing 'Lipton Currency Notes'. The store was a huge success and quickly expanded. By 1880, Lipton had 20 stores, and by 1890 he had 300. He was a household name throughout Britain, renowned for his innovative retailing and promotional techniques.

Rather than resting on his laurels, Lipton moved on to new things. As well as entering the Americas Cup, something he would win five times between 1899 and 1930, he decided to get into the tea business.

He felt there was an opportunity to make tea universally accessible, with guaranteed quality at acceptable prices. He chose to bypass the traditional trading and wholesale distribution channels (most UK tea-trading was focused in London's Mincing Lane). At that time, tea was a drink for the wealthy, with the price around three shillings a pound (15p). Lipton would price his tea at the equivalent of one shilling seven pence a pound (7.5p).

Tea had traditionally arrived in crates and was sold loose, but Lipton would change that as his tea was now pre-packed at multiple weight options and standardized to guarantee quality. Later, Lipton would be the first brand to sell tea leaves in tea bags.

The arrival of his first tea shipment was done in traditional Lipton style with an accompanying parade of brass bands and bagpipers.

The next big change happened when Lipton went on 'vacation' to Australia. In fact, he never planned on going to Australia: the story was a cover for a trip to Ceylon (Sri Lanka). There a recent blight had ruined the English coffee planters, and the survivors were now planting tea. With land prices low, Lipton spotted another opportunity, and bought five of the bankrupt plantations. This and his subsequent acquisition of about a further dozen sites allowed him to unveil a new slogan: "Direct from the Tea Gardens to the Teapot."

In 1893, he officially established the Thomas J Lipton Co and the Lipton brand of teas.

Lipton® teas were an immediate success in the United Kingdom and the United States where, for his headquarters, he chose a warehouse in Hoboken, New Jersey. True to form, he was not backwards in announcing his arrival, and built a huge Lipton's Tea sign that could clearly be read from any point in New York harbour.

In recognition of his exceptional contribution to the country, Thomas Lipton was knighted by Queen Victoria in 1898, and became Sir Thomas Lipton at the age of 48.

Lipton® is now the world's leading tea brand, sold in more than 150 countries.

And the moral is, if people don't know about your brand, how will they know whether to buy it or not? How can you ensure maximum publicity for your brand?

30. HOW A RUSSIAN HELPED CREATE AN ICONIC AMERICAN BRAND

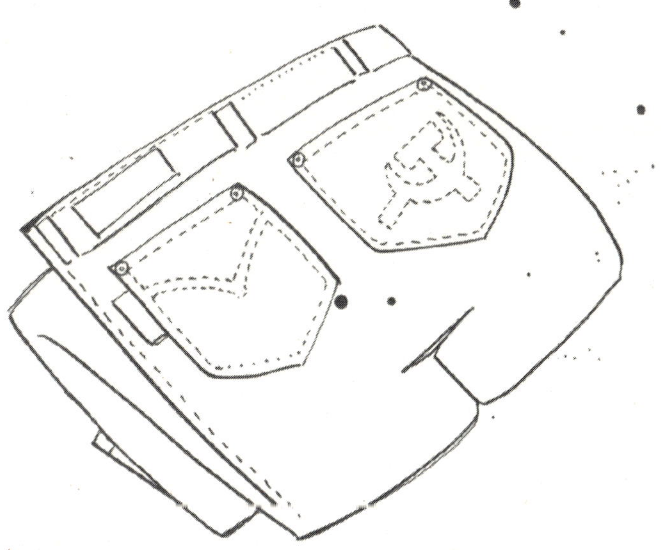

One of the most famous American brands of all time wouldn't exist today if it weren't for the Russians, or more particularly one specific Russian – Jacob Youphes.

Those of you who guessed the brand as Levi 501s and know your jeans history would be forgiven for being confused – didn't Levi Strauss create 501s?

Well the correct answer is yes …and no.

501s were, and are, produced by Levi Strauss. But the distinctive and differentiating features of the brass rivets and the double orange threaded stitching were Jacob Davis's ideas.

Davis doesn't sound very Russian, but then again he wasn't always Jacob Davis. Jacob was born Jacob Youphes in 1831 in Riga, then part of the Russian Empire, now the capital of Latvia, where he trained and worked as a tailor.

In 1854, he emigrated to the United States where, shortly after arriving in New York, he decided to change his name to Jacob Davis.

After a number of years travelling and working in various states, he finally settled in Reno where he opened a tailor's shop in 1869.

Much of his trade was in practical hard-wearing items such as tents, horse blankets and wagon covers for the railway workers on the Central Pacific Railroad. The fabrics he worked with were a heavy-duty cotton "duck" cloth, and a heavy-duty cotton "denim" cloth.

He bought this latter fabric from a certain Levi Strauss & Co, a dry goods company in San Francisco.

In December 1870, Davis was asked by a customer to make a pair of strong "working pants" for her husband who was a woodcutter.

Thinking how to create suitably robust trousers, he opted for duck cloth and had the idea to apply a technique he was using on his tents and wagon covers. He decided to reinforce potentially weaker areas with copper rivets, putting them in the seams and pockets of his new trousers.

His customer and her husband were delighted, and told their friends and colleagues. Word spread throughout the labourers along the railroad. Davis was soon making more and more of his working pants in both duck cotton and, as early as 1871, in denim cotton too.

Realizing the potential value of his reinforced jeans concept, and recognizing he would need help and capital if his new pants were going to be a success, he approached Levi Strauss in 1872, asking for his financial backing in the filing of a patent application.

Strauss too could see the potential, and on 20 May 1873, US Patent No 139,121 for "improvements in fastening pocket openings" was issued in the name of Jacob W Davis, and Levi Strauss and Company.

That same year, Davis started sewing a double orange threaded stitched design onto the back pocket of the jeans to distinguish them from those made by his competitors. This feature would be registered too: US Trade Mark No 1,339,254.

Strauss set up a new and sizeable tailor's shop in San Francisco for the production of Davis's working pants, and asked Jacob and his family to come to the city and run it.

As demand continued to grow, the shop was superseded by a manufacturing plant that Davis was asked to manage. Davis continued to work there for the remainder of his life, overseeing production of the work pants, as well as other lines including work shirts and overalls.

The brand however resided with Strauss and, over time, Jacob's contribution has become less well-known.

These days, the Russian's contribution is known only by fashion and brand historians ... and now you.

And the moral is, innovation in one market often borrows from other markets. Where could you be borrowing ideas from?

31. HOW AN OVER-WORKED BAKER, THE US NAVY AND THE EXECUTIVE'S WIFE HELPED CREATE THE GREATEST KITCHEN AID EVER

Herbert Johnston, an engineer at the Hobart Manufacturing Company, was a curious man – or rather he was a man who was constantly curious. He was the kind of engineer who liked using his practical skills to solve other people's problems.

So, when in 1908 he saw an over-worked baker mixing bread dough with nothing but an iron spoon and brute force, he thought there must be a better way.

It took him nearly *seven* years to develop an 80-quart electrical stand mixer. But once it was launched, sales grew rapidly – saving bakers' arms up and down the country.

It came to the notice of the US Navy procurement department who ordered mixers for two new Tennessee-class battleships, the California and the Tennessee, as well as the US Navy's first dreadnought battleship, the South Carolina. By 1917, the stand mixer had become "regular equipment" on all US Navy ships.

The product's overwhelming success prompted Johnson and the other Hobart engineers to think about the potential for a smaller model that might be used in home kitchens. World War I interfered, and while the battleships benefited from the mixers, the American public had to wait until peacetime returned.

It wasn't until 1919 that the Model H-5, the first stand mixer for the home, was introduced. It came not only with an array of attachments, but with a new brand name too. According to the brand's official history, the name was given to it by one of the Hobart executive's wives who is supposed to have exclaimed: "I don't care what you call it, but I know it's the best kitchen aid I've ever had!"

The KitchenAid trademark was quickly registered with the US Patent Office.

The H-5 was also the first in a long line of KitchenAid stand mixers that utilized a "planetary action": a revolutionary design that rotated the beater in one direction while moving it around the bowl in the opposite path.

It wasn't a small unit though, standing about 26 inches (33cm) high and weighing approximately 65lbs (29.5kg).

Many retailers were initially hesitant to carry the unique product, so the company turned to its own, largely female, sales force, who set out to sell the 65lb H-5 door to door. They gave in-home demonstrations to groups of women, demonstrating how the machine could mix, beat, cut, cream, slice, chop, grind and strain, and sales quickly grew.

In 1927, the Model G stand mixer was introduced. Lighter and more compact than the H-5, it sold 20,000 units in its first three years on the market. Early adopters of the Model G included John Barrymore, Henry Ford, and Ginger Rogers.

Then in the 1930s, the company hired Egmont Arens to design three new, more affordable stand mixer models. Arens was the art editor of *Vanity Fair*, as well as being a world-renowned artist, designer, and "industrial humaneer" championing a consumer-centric approach to product design and packaging.

His client list included GE, Fairchild Aircraft, the General American Transportation Company, and indeed the Hobart company for whom he had designed a meat slicer.

Arens' design for the 4½-quart-capacity Model K45 was sleek and futuristic, far ahead of its time. It remains virtually unchanged to this day. It was released in 1937 to huge success. All KitchenAid components are compatible with the front attachment hub of every mixer made since that day.

One final and famous innovation wasn't actually introduced until 1955, when at the Atlantic City Housewares Show, KitchenAid unveiled a range of colours including

Petal Pink, Sunny Yellow, Island Green, Satin Chrome, and Antique Copper.

So, if like Herbert Johnston you are naturally curious and had wondered about the origins of your KitchenAid, now you know.

And the moral is, a brand can be built on solving people's problems. What problems do you know that haven't been solved yet (or could be solved better)?

32. NAPOLEON, TWO MATHEMATICALLY MINDED MINISTERS AND THE BIRTH OF THE INSURANCE FUNDS INDUSTRY

Napoleon is credited with many achievements, but most lists don't include his contribution to one of Britain's most famous financial brands.

On its website, Scottish Widows traces its origins back to March 1812, when a number of prominent Scotsmen gathered in the Royal Exchange Coffee Rooms in Edinburgh. It was a turbulent time for the UK, with not only the Napoleonic wars, but war against the US looming on the horizon.

An historic meeting was held to discuss setting up "a general fund for securing provisions to widows, sisters and other female relatives". This fund would prevent them from being plunged into poverty on the death of the fund holders during and after the Napoleonic Wars.

The discussions and planning took some time. It wasn't until 1815, the year of Napoleon's ultimate defeat at Waterloo, that the Scottish Widows Fund and Life Assurance Society opened its doors as Scotland's first mutual life office.

There is, however, a story behind the story: how the origins of the brand, and indeed the industry, can be traced even further back in history, to two Church of Scotland ministers. They deserve the credit for inventing the first 'true' insurance fund, way back in 1744.

Robert Wallace and his friend Alexander Webster were men of vision. The two ministers were unhappy with the way the wives and children of their fellow clergymen were often treated when the men of their households died. They were generally left at the mercy of the fellow ministers, and despite relying on Christian benefactors, they were often left homeless and without any income.

In response to this problem, Wallace and Webster came up with an ingenious plan, which is now recognized as the first insurance fund in history. They proposed that each of their church's ministers pay a small portion of his income into a fund, which was invested. Then, if a minister died, his widow would receive dividends from the fund's profits, allowing her to live comfortably for the rest of her life.

The key question was how much each minister needed to pay in so the fund had enough money to deliver on its obligations. Webster and Wallace realized they must try to predict how many ministers would die every year, how many widows and orphans would be left behind, and how many years the widows would live on for.

Recognizing their limitations, they contacted Colin Maclaurin, professor of mathematics at the University of Edinburgh.

The three of them collected data on the ages at which ministers had died, and used it to calculate how many were likely to pass away in any given year.

Through their calculations, they concluded that there would be 930 living Scottish Presbyterian ministers at any given time, and that an average of 27 ministers would die each year, 18 of whom would leave widows. Five of those who did not leave widows would, however, leave orphaned children. And two of those survived by widows would also be out-lived by children from previous marriages who had not yet reached the age of 16.

They then further calculated how long it would be before those widows either died or remarried, as both eventualities caused payments to cease.

The final calculations suggested that by contributing £2, 12 shillings and 2 pence annually (equivalent to £2.61 today), they would guarantee widows receive £10 a year (a living income in those days). With additional contributions, a minister could guarantee his widow would receive a greater sum each year.

The bottom line was that by 1765 the fund – Provision for the Widows and Children of the Ministers of the Church of Scotland – should have capital totalling £58,348.

Records show that the capital in 1765 was in fact £58,347, just £1 out.

And the moral is that a brand may have a noble purpose but needs a sensible business model to succeed. How strong is your brand's underlying business model?

Footnote: The famous caped Scottish Widow didn't appear as the brand's icon until 1986, when she made her debut in a television advert directed by David Bailey. The 'living logo' was created to be an icon that confronted all the negative values associated with the word 'widow', and presented the positive values – strength, reliability, integrity, innovation and heritage. Her impact was immediate, Scottish Widows became a household name and 'awareness' increased from 34% to 92%.

33. HOW A STANDARD LAMP INSPIRED ONE OF THE FASTEST GROWING ONLINE FASHION BRANDS

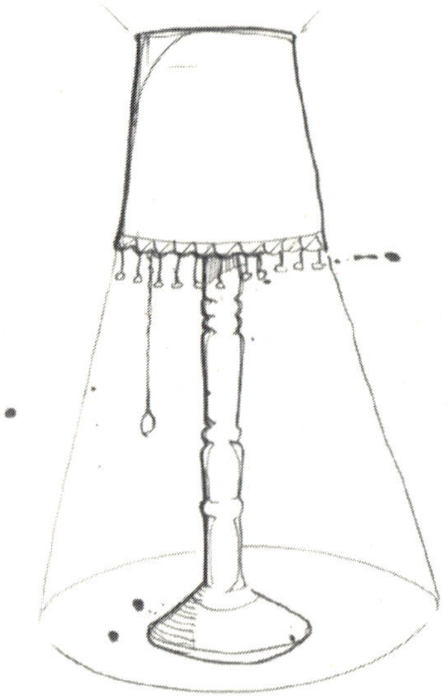

Inspiration, like fashion, comes in all shapes and sizes.

The inspiration for the hugely successful on-line fashion brand ASOS came from a standard lamp. Co-founder Nick Robertson mentions that he and his partner, Quentin Griffiths, "read a stat back in 1999 that when the US programme *Friends* aired, NBC got 4,000 calls about some standard lamp in one of their apartments, asking where it could be purchased. So that was the real idea behind the business".

The thinking behind the brand was a logical development from this: "Anything that gets exposure in a film or TV programme creates desire among the public, so we based the shop around that."

Their choice of brand name for their launch in June 2000 followed naturally – As Seen On Screen.

Initially, the focus wasn't just on fashion. But that changed with one of their earliest hires, Lorri Penn, who they headhunted from Arcadia (Sir Philip Green's UK retail group, which includes Topshop and Dorothy Perkins).

Penn argued that fashion was the way forward.

"It wasn't until our first buyer came in, who was a fashion buyer, that we were pushed in that direction," Nick says. "Fashion is where we got the most returns for the business. Rather than saying 'here's a standard top', we could say 'here's a top that Jennifer Aniston wore in *Friends*'."

The founders agreed to back Lorri's judgment and focused on fashion, moving As Seen On Screen from a website for all celebrity-linked products to fashion only.

Sales have grown from £250,000 to over £200m. From a handful of employees, ASOS now has over 1,000, and the range of products on its site, though all fashion related, runs to over 35,000.

Where once ASOS followed, now it leads. From merely replicating celebrity fashion, it has come so far that it is now helping set celebrity fashion trends. ASOS own-label creations are now worn by celebrities from Rihanna to Kate Hudson.

And the moral is that inspiration for a new brand can come from anywhere, at any time. Do you have your eyes and ears working 24/7?

34. R A L S B E B C = 14 (AT LEAST)

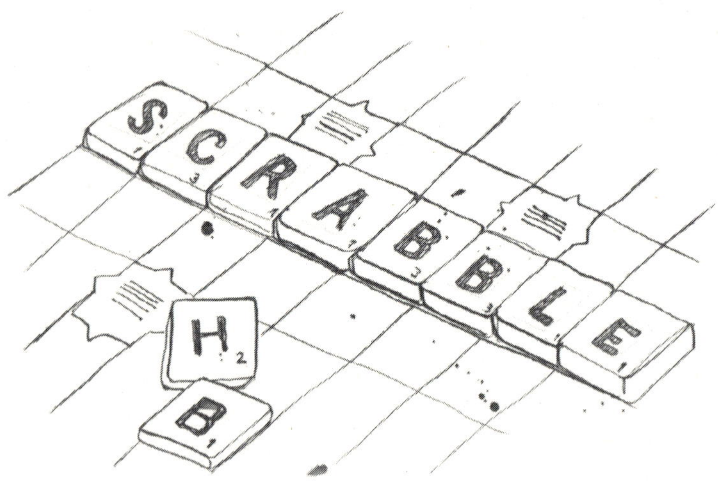

America's Great Depression caused untold misery. But the necessity of trying to feed your family often drove people on. I have already written the tale of how Charles Darrow developed what was to become Monopoly after losing his job at a sales company. However, he was not the only person for whom necessity was the mother of invention.

In 1933, Alfred Mosher Butts lost his job as an architect, so decided to try his hand at developing a board game.

He set about it methodically and, although he might not have known it, he followed many of the principles of best practice in innovation – analyse the market, identify the best opportunity area, develop something new that fits into that space, prototype it and test it.

He began by analysing the set of current board games. Sitting in his apartment in Queens, New York City, he determined that there were three types of board games – move games like chess, number games such as bingo, and word games, of which he could think of just one example, Anagrams.

Having identified word games as his opportunity area, he decided he wanted to create a game that combined the vocabulary skills of crossword puzzles and anagrams, with an additional element of chance.

He analysed the front pages of newspapers including the *New York Herald*, to assess the frequency with which each letter in the alphabet appeared. He used this information to decide how many tiles of each letter there should be and how many points each letter ought to be worth.

The game, which Butts originally called Lexico, was the result. In its first few years, it went under a variety of different names including 'It' and 'Criss-Cross words'.

The first prototypes had boards that were hand-drawn using Butts' architectural drafting equipment, reproduced by blueprinting and pasting on folding checkerboards. The tiles were also hand-lettered, then glued to quarter-inch balsa and cut to match the squares on the board.

His wife Nina was an ex-schoolteacher and his first 'guinea pig'. She beat Alfred at his own game – he claimed he was never any good at spelling. It has been reported that Nina once notched up nearly 300 points using the word 'quixotic' across two triple-word scores.

Soon the couple were gathering friends and neighbours to play in the hall of the local Methodist church, but the game stubbornly remained a local hit.

By mid-1934, Butts had sold just 84 handmade sets at a loss of $20. Every major games' manufacturer turned it down, and his application for a patent met the same fate.

Luckily for Butts, the economy began to pick up and he was able to resume his old job at the architectural firm.

He and his friends still continued to play the game, and sold a few sets over the years.

One was bought by James Brunot who, when he retired from his day job in 1948, approached Butts with an offer to make and sell the game. Butts agreed.

Brunot came up with a new name, 'Scrabble', and lodged a successful copyright application.

Unfortunately the game was not an immediate success. In 1949, Brunot made 2,400 sets and lost $450.

Over the next two to three years the brand grew, but only slowly.

Then, the brand had a stroke of luck. In 1952, the president of Macy's department store happened to see a Scrabble game in progress while holidaying in Florida. He liked what he saw and decided to stock some in his store.

The game took off almost immediately and Macy's was soon selling 6,000 sets a week.

By 1952, Brunot realized he could not make the games fast enough to meet the growing interest, so licensed a well-known game manufacturer, Selchow & Righter, to market and distribute them in the United States and Canada.

In 1972, Selchow & Righter bought Brunot out. Brunot received $1.3 million and Butts got $265,000.

Today, more than 150 million Scrabble sets have been sold in 29 languages. Scrabble has become a cultural icon, appearing in episodes of *Seinfeld* and *The Simpsons*, and in lyrics sung by Kylie Minogue and Sting.

And the moral is that not all successful brands are overnight sensations. Are you giving your new brands enough time?

Footnote 1: Butts used some of his earnings to buy the farmhouse in upstate New York where he had grown up, and there, while in his late seventies, he created a second game. It too was a word game. His choice of name, however, showed that he had more to learn as an innovator. He called his new invention "Alfred's Other Game".

Footnote 2: Butts was a resident of Jackson Heights, New York, when he invented Scrabble. There is now a special street sign at 35th Avenue and 81st Street in Jackson Heights that is stylized using letters, with their values, in Scrabble script to commemorate this association.

35. ABSOLUTELY FABULIS? NO. FABULOUSLY FAB, ABSOLUTELY! – HOW TWO WRONGS LED TO A RIGHT

Are you willing to admit you're wrong? Not once, but twice?

Are you brave enough to go to your million-dollar backers and tell them you've made a mistake?

Luckily for Jason Goldberg and Bradford Shellhammer, they were. Even more luckily, their backers were willing not only to listen, but also to agree to the changes.

Jason and Bradford got together in 2010 to start a company they called Fabulis. Their aim was to create a social network for gay men, but competition from the likes of Facebook and Grindr meant uptake was limited. They quickly realized there was no gap in the market.

So, in December 2011, the pair decided to change direction and Fabulis became Fab.com, a daily deals site for gay men. Their new ambition was to become Groupon for gays. They raised $1.75 million from First Round Capital, The Washington Post Company, Baroda Ventures and Zelkova Ventures, to add to the $1.25 million they had already raised in angel funding.

Fab.com got off to a reasonable start, reaching several thousand customers and earning tens of thousands of dollars in revenue in just 20 days of sales. But for the ambitious duo, it wasn't big enough. Interviewed by *Inc.* in 2012, they recall: "We just didn't see how that [it] had a path to become a huge business."

Looking more closely at initial figures, they saw that less than 1% of the most popular selling items were gay specific, and, in fact, over half of the people making purchases weren't gay; they just appreciated the selection of products and discounts.

The pair sat down again, and this time asked themselves what was to prove an inspirational question: "If we could do anything, what would we do? Which was a great exercise for us and we kind of had this decision matrix of looking at three things; one is, what are we most passionate about? The second is, what could we be the best in the world at? The third is, could we do it in a great market where there's a big opportunity? And every answer of those questions came down to design, design, design," Jason explained.

The certainty of their answer spurred them into action, and a dramatic three weeks followed: "We went from 10 employees here in New York, to three. We really wanted to focus just on the people who were gonna be part of the next phase of the business. The second thing was we went and got our board of directors to, very quickly, say 'hey, we're behind this and we support this move'. The third thing was we immediately shut down the old site."

The clarity of their answer gave them focus and direction: "We immediately took this mentality that we were gonna do one thing, do that one thing better than anyone else in the world, and we don't want to be distracted at all by anything else besides our one thing. We are just focusing on design. That's all we do is design. Every day we wake up, and all we think about is design. And basically [we] went from dinners in February where we said we're gonna change the business, to shutting down the site in March, to launching some initial features in April, to launching ourselves in June to one and a half million members."

Looking at the business now, they can smile. And they think part of their success is down to making others smile too. "We're growing fast because we make people smile every day. We're breathing kind of freshness, colour into an otherwise, a kind of fairly black and white, kinda boring e-commerce world. And every day we delight people with the daily dose of design, and it's just stuff that makes people smile."

And the moral is that sometimes you need to admit your first idea wasn't right and needs to be adapted. Do you learn from mistakes and make necessary changes?

36. TEACH YOURSELF – THE REDBUS STORY

It was approaching Diwali in 2005, and Phanindra Sama was trying to get a bus ticket from Bangalore, where he was working for Texas Instruments, to his hometown Hyderabad.

His regular travel agent didn't have any, nor did the many others he approached. Tickets for buses in India are traditionally sold in kiosks, but none of those Phani visited had any left.

Disappointed, he returned to his flat in Koramangala, which he shared with six friends, all of whom had studied engineering at BITS Pilani.

There, after cursing his bad luck, he got to wondering whether there might have been a travel agent somewhere in city that might have had one ticket left. Had that ticket remained unsold? In which case everybody – he, the travel agent, and the bus operator – had missed an opportunity. How many others like it had been missed too?

Phani had an idea.

He put it to his friends. Could the internet be the answer: a website where bus operators post their seat inventory, and customers book them online?

It was simple. It was brilliant. But there was a problem. "We didn't know anything about the bus industry. We didn't even know anything about software or websites. I was designing microchips and he (Charan Padmaraju one of his flatmates who would go on to be one of the co-founders of redBus) was doing embedded design. We actually bought textbooks on how to write software and started learning," Phani says.

They met with various people – bus operators, passengers and venture capitalists – to gauge how well the concept could do. Everyone they spoke to was excited.

They then put together a business plan and presented it to TiE – The Indus Entrepreneurs, Bangalore Chapter – whose members act as mentors. The idea didn't need much selling to TiE either.

The founders decided to quit their jobs, and the real journey began.

India has more than 5,000 intercity bus operators with 5 to 500 buses each. They were used to dealing with traditional brick-and-mortar travel agents, so changing their mindset wasn't easy. Along with developing the website, it took a few months for everything to fall into place.

The name redBus is a blend and was born from a bit of borrowed inspiration: "We wanted a colour in the name of our site. And an easy, short word is always best for the web.

'Red' was the shortest. It also denotes energy, youthfulness. I was then reading Richard Branson's autobiography and that was hugely inspiring, and his Virgin [brand] was red," Phani says.

Finally, they were ready. And in August 2006, they took their first booking. Perhaps surprisingly there was as much nervousness as there was excitement at the website's office. Would the conductor allow the traveller in? He might never have seen a computer printed bus ticket before.

"We were scared," recalls Phani. "So we all went to the bus stand to board the customer, who was a lady from Infosys [an Indian information technology company] going to Tirupati. It was an auspicious beginning."

Since then, the brand has gone from strength to strength. They now have 1,500+ bus operators and 80,000 routes covered. They sell over a million tickets a month. In 2012, *Fast Company* named redBus among the world's 50 most innovative companies, alongside Apple, Facebook and Google.

And the moral is, if you want to create something new, you need to be willing to learn new skills. Are your ideas being held back because you are too set in your ways?

37. THE BEST JOB IN THE WORLD

Hotel Chocolat is perhaps one of the most vertically integrated brands around.

It came into existence in 2003 as the latest iteration of a business that Angus Thirlwell and Peter Harris started in 1993, selling mints as MMC. A few years later, they moved into the market they were truly passionate about – chocolate, and rebranded as Geneva Chocolates.

Their stated objective was to make chocolate that really excited the senses, and to make that chocolate widely available. To that end, they start selling chocolates online, becoming one of the UK's earliest e-tailers, predating the likes of Amazon and eBay. Another change of name followed, this time to Choc Express.

In 1998, they launched the Chocolate Tasting Club, a subscription-based service that allows members to receive, taste and test chocolates every month. It is still running and has around 100,000 members.

In 2003, Choc Express rebranded as Hotel Chocolat, and in 2004 launched its first retail store in the centre of … London? New York? Paris? Geneva? – no, Watford.

It was a showcase for their unique take on chocolate, an approach that didn't follow the accepted rules of the market…

Those rules said that a slab of chocolate should be regular and divided into bite-sized pieces, Angus and Peter made curvy and iconic Giant Slabs.

When they started making Easter Eggs, they were advised by experts to make them as thin as possible and put the chocolates on the outside. They did the opposite – making really thick shells with all of the chocolates hidden inside for extra excitement.

Long before the trend for more cocoa and less sugar in chocolate, their house-grade milk chocolate was 50% cocoa, and their white chocolate was 36% cocoa, well above the average percentages back then.

Despite breaking all these rules, the store was a huge success and others quickly followed across the UK, and later in the US and Europe.

In 2005, a customer sent Angus a book she had found while tidying her husband's study. She thought he might be interested; little did she know how interested.

It was a 1920 edition of Cocoa & Chocolate, Their History from Plantation to Consumer. It told the history of cocoa growing in the West Indies. It struck a chord with Angus, who had not only spent part of his childhood there, but wanted to more closely link the brand with its roots – literally and metaphorically.

An intensive search began. A search that included several islands, before Angus and Peter found The Rabot Estate in Saint Lucia. They both fell in love with the estate and bought it in April 2006.

The brand now grew some of its cocoa, made its own chocolates, developed its own recipes and sold them in its own shops. But this vertical extension of the brand was only just beginning.

In 2011, Hotel Chocolat lived up to its name and opened its own guest house – the Boucan Hotel. It sits on the edge of the Rabot Estate perched high up in the Piton Mountains. The luxury hotel and spa has six lodges and a cocoa-inspired Boucan Restaurant. It too is a success, and people fly in from around the world to enjoy the food.

In 2014, Angus and Peter decided to bring the cocoa plantation experience to Britain, and launched two new restaurants in London and Leeds.

Not content with that, they also launched their School of Chocolate at Cocoa Vaults in Covent Garden, London, where they offer chocolate-making sessions, tasting events and bespoke parties for everyone, from chocolate-loving kids to cocoa-addicted corporate teams.

In 2015, they published their first cookbook *A New Way of Cooking with Chocolate*, so now anyone can have a go at making award-winning dishes in their own homes.

Not surprisingly, Angus loves his job. "I count myself as one of the luckiest people around – to work every day in a business that lives by my obsessions for chocolate, true creativity and honest ingredients, and which also has a link back to my childhood in the West Indies through our cocoa estate in Saint Lucia."

It is a job that is the envy of millions of chocolate lovers.

And the moral is that brands can be built by turning a passion into a purpose. How could your passion become the basis for a new brand?

NAMING AND IDENTITIES

Brand naming and brand design are two different but equally important marketing disciplines. They are at the heart of many classical definitions of a brand. For example, Philip Kotler in *Managing Markets* defines a brand as: "A name, term, symbol or design, or a combination of them, which is intended to signify the goods or services of one seller or group of sellers, and to differentiate them from those of competitors."

Naming has come a long way. We take the strategies and stories behind brand names for granted. In fact, they are often a delightful mix of the rational and the strange. They provide inspiration and ideas for anyone faced with the challenge of naming their own brand.

Beauty is in the eye of the beholder, or so they say, but the best designs do more than just identify a brand – they signify meaning. From brand logos to brand icons, the tales here show the imagination and application of designers' skills to a commercial end. Stories about the usage of imagery, colour, even a dead lion, make interesting reading – and hopefully provide a little guidance too.

38. INTRODUCING MISS WHITE FROM LONDON

How many clues do you need to guess the brand?

Her surname is White.
She lives in London.
Her birthday is 1 November.
She has a twin sister named Mimmy.
Her favourite food is apple pie.
Her favourite word is friendship
Her favourite subjects in school are English, music and art.
She is five apples tall and weighs three apples.
She is in the third grade, but when school's out she travels the world making new friends.
She is bright, kind-hearted, and loves the outdoors.

She has no mouth.

She first appeared in 1974 and doesn't seem to have aged a day since then.

She is none other than the worldwide mega brand Hello Kitty.

Kitty's story actually begins in 1962, when Shintaro Tsuji founded Sanrio and began selling rubber sandals with flowers painted on them.

Over time, Tsuji noticed that when a cute design was added to the range of merchandise, sales and profits increased. So he started to hire cartoonists to design cute characters for him.

In 1974, Tsuji commissioned Yuko Shimizu to create a new character. The brief was for a "British" character because at the time, in the mid-1970s, foreign countries and in particular, Britain, were considered trendy in Japan. Sanrio's motto is "social communication", and Tsuji's other request was that the new brand name should reflect that.

Shimizu came up with a drawing of a white Japanese Bobtail cat that had a red bow in its hair and was wearing blue overalls. She got the name 'Kitty' from Lewis Carroll's *Through the Looking-Glass*, where Alice's cat is called Kitty.

To reflect social communication, Shimizu first considered "Hi Kitty" before settling on "Hello" to capture the friendly nature required.

A distinctive feature of Hello Kitty is the lack of a mouth. Spokespeople for Sanrio have given slightly different explanations for the omission over time. At one time they said they wanted people to "project their feelings onto the character" and "be happy or sad together with Hello Kitty".

The character's first appearance on an item was a vinyl coin purse in Japan, where she was pictured sitting between a bottle of milk and a goldfish bowl. She first appeared in the United States in 1976.

Originally aimed at pre-teen girls, Hello Kitty's market has broadened considerably to include adult consumers. She can now be found on a huge variety of products, ranging from school supplies to fashion accessories and high-end consumer products.

Several Hello Kitty TV series have been produced, and she is the main character at the two Japanese Sanrio theme parks, Harmonyland and the indoor Sanrio Puroland.

In 2014, Hello Kitty was estimated to be delivering $7 billion a year, interestingly all without any advertising.

And the moral is, a brand can benefit from a back story. What is the story behind your brand?

39. WHEN DARK AND BROKEN

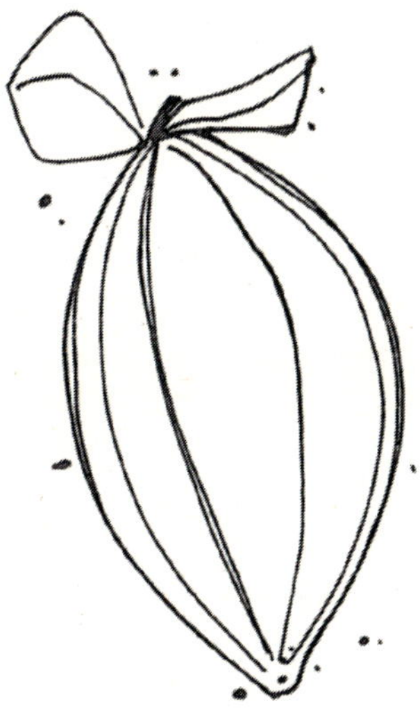

"A bottle which a person could recognize even if they felt it in the dark, and so shaped that, even if broken, a person could tell at a glance what it was." That was the brief that was issued by the Coca-Cola Company when it launched a competition among its bottle suppliers to create a new and distinctive bottle shape in 1915.

At one of the suppliers, the Root Glass Company of Terre Haute, Indiana, Chapman J Root, president, decided to delegate the project to members of his supervisory staff, including the company auditor T Clyde Edwards, the plant superintendent Alexander Samuelsson, and Earl R Dean, a bottle designer and the supervisor of the bottle moulding room.

After much thought, they came up with the idea of basing the bottle's design on one of Coca-Cola's key ingredients. In particular, the coca leaf or the kola nut. There was one slight snag, none of the team knew what either of those ingredients looked like.

Dean and Edwards decided to go to the Emeline Fairbanks Memorial Library, but their search was unsuccessful as neither were able to find any information about coca or kola.

With time running out, Dean found and was inspired by a picture of the gourd-shaped cocoa pod in the *Encyclopædia Britannica*. He made a rough sketch of the pod and returned to the plant to show Root how he could transform the pod shape into a bottle. Root liked the idea, and gave Dean his approval to develop it further.

A second complication now faced Dean. There was an upcoming scheduled maintenance of the mould-making machinery, so Dean needed to work at speed. Over the next 24 hours, Dean sketched out a concept drawing which was approved by Root the next morning. Dean then managed to create a bottle mould and produce a small number of the prototype bottles before the glass-moulding machinery was turned off.

A design patent was issued on the bottle in November 1915.

At the 1916 bottlers' convention, Dean's "contour" bottle was chosen as the winning design, but the prototypes never made it to production. The bottle's middle diameter was larger than the base diameter, and this made it unstable as it went down the conveyor belts. Dean resolved this final issue by decreasing the bottle's middle diameter, and the bottle made it to the market later in 1916.

By 1920, the contour bottle became the standard for the Coca-Cola Company. Today, the contour Coca-Cola bottle remains one of the most recognized packages on the planet..."even in the dark".

As a reward for his efforts, Dean was offered a choice between a $500 bonus or a lifetime job at the Root Glass Company. He chose the lifetime job, which he kept until the Owens-Illinois Glass Company bought out the Root Glass Company in the mid-1930s.

And the moral is, packaging can be your silent salesman. Are you doing enough with your packaging?

40. A ROARING SUCCESS

The famous logo of Metro-Goldwyn Mayer is not one lion, but a whole pride of them.

In 1917, Samuel Goldwyn asked studio publicist Howard Dietz to design a logo for Goldwyn Picture Corporation. In the end, Dietz chose to use a lion as the studio's mascot, paying tribute to his alma mater, Columbia University and its athletic team, the Lions. The specific inspiration was said to be the school's fight song *Roar, Lion, Roar*. Deitz also wrote the Latin motto *Ars Gratia Artis*, which means "Art for Art's Sake".

When Goldwyn Pictures merged with Metro Pictures Corporation and Louis B. Mayer Pictures, the newly formed MGM retained the lion logo.

Slats (1917-1928) was MGM's first lion. He was born at Dublin Zoo and was trained by Volney Phifer, Hollywood's premier animal trainer of the time. The pair toured the country to promote MGM's launch and became close. So much so that when Slats died in 1936, Phifer had the body sent to his farm and buried him there, marking the grave with a granite slab and a pine tree to "hold down the lion's spirit".

Telly (1928-1932) and Coffee (1932-1935) were briefly used in Technicolor tests, but both had short-lived careers.

Jackie (1928-1956) was the next in line and was the first MGM lion to be heard as well as seen. He introduced MGM's first sound production, *White Shadows in the South Seas*, with his roar. Jackie was also a performer in his own right, appearing in over 100 movies.

Some people said that Jackie was unlucky; he was involved in two train wrecks, an earthquake, a boat sinking, an explosion at the studio, and a plane crash that left him stranded in the Arizona wilderness for several days. On the other hand and perhaps not surprisingly he survived all of these, chance was on his side and he deserved his nickname "the Lucky."

Tanner followed Jackie and reigned throughout what is now known as the 'Golden Age of Hollywood'. Tanner was used on almost all Technicolor MGM films from 1934–1956, and on the cartoons from late 1935–1958 with one or two notable exceptions. These included *The Wizard of Oz* (1939) which had Oz scenes in colour, but the opening and closing credits (and indeed the Kansas scenes) in sepia-toned black-and-white, so they used the old black-and-white footage of Jackie.

Tanner was described as MGM's "angriest" lion by Koontz because he snarled all the time.

George (1956-1958) followed Tanner, but had a relatively short-lived stint and doesn't appear to have made that much of an impression.

Starting in 1957, Leo is not only the current lion, but also MGM's longest-serving lion. Like Jackie, Leo's performances weren't limited to his appearance in the logo. He appeared in several *Tarzan* movies, the *Tarzan* TV series, and other films as well.

Though known universally as Leo, this may or may not have been his actual name. He was purchased from an animal dealer, Henry Treffich, and it seems no-one knew what he was actually called. Leo was the name used by someone at the studio, and it stuck.

Leo has sometimes been replaced by some more humorous stand-ins over the years, including the Marx Brothers, a lion with blood-dripping fangs in *The Fearless Vampire Killers*, a croaking frog, Mimsie the Cat in *The Mary Tyler Moore Show*, a meowing Tom in *Tom and Jerry* and Animal in *The Great Muppet Caper*.

And the moral is, the best brand identities can live on and on if constantly updated. Is your brand identity strong enough to stand the test of time?

41. THE SWALLOW, THE STEAMSHIPS AND THE JAGUAR

The Swallow Sidecar Company was established by Sir William Lyons in 1922, and originally built its name making motorcycle sidecars. The name Swallow was chosen because it evoked speed and grace.

A few years later, on the back of his success with sidecars, the ambitious Sir William decided to broaden Swallow's range, and started using the coach-building expertise of his designers and workers to make dynamic and exciting bodies for the normally sedate Austin Sevens. The cars with their bright colours and chrome trims stood out from the staid cars of the time, which were normally green or black.

He persuaded car-sellers Bertie Henly and Frank Hough, who had a showroom at 91 Great Portland Street, London, to take them. In fact, Henly ordered 500. They were known as SS1 and SS2, and sold well.

When it came to the launch of the all-new SS 100, Sir William wanted a new and evocative name for his latest offering. After asking his advertising agency, Nelson, for suggestions, Sir William chose 'Jaguar'. The name was introduced in September 1935, and the cars were known as SS Jaguars.

With the onset of World War II, the factories and plants were put to military use by the British government, and car production came to a standstill. The sidecar side of the business was still active, and it manufactured over 10,000 units for the British army's motor corps.

After the war, when car production resumed, saloons and drophead coupés, the latter referred to as Mark IV's, were the first to come off the assembly line.

The management at what was still officially known as SS Cars Ltd thought it would be best to change its name to Jaguar Cars Ltd. There were too many negative connotations with the initials SS.

Some years later, reflecting on the name change, Sir William said that he felt it was appropriate, not only because it represented the feline grace and elegance, power and agility that set his cars apart, but a Jaguar "was the closest thing we can create to something that is alive."

And the moral is, some of the best brand names are associative. How will you choose the name for your next new launch?

42. THE SPIRIT OF THE BLITZ BOTTLED

Fuller's Brewery is an independent family brewery. It is based in Chiswick, West London, on a site where beer has been brewed for over 350 years.

In 2013 it started a new campaign for one of its beers.

"In the 50s we created new ale.
Rich, smooth and wonderfully balanced.
We just needed a name.
There was no twitter back then, but we asked around London for suggestions all the same, and one in particular was inspired.
A flower.
But not any old flower.

'London Pride' (or Saxifraga x urbium to be precise).
A tough little perennial that grew during the Blitz, covering the rubble like tiny beacons of hope.
A homage to the city's indomitable spirit, and a fitting name for our ale.
So thank you London."

And the moral is, brand names can come from anywhere, including your customers. How will you develop your next new brand name?

Source : No Wall flower – London Pride advertising campaign 2013 (Created by The Corner London)

43. BIG, GREEN AND NOT VERY JOLLY

Who would have thought that a tall, lumbering and scowling caveman carrying a huge pea pod would become one of the world's leading advertising icons?

Luckily for the Jolly Green Giant, The Minnesota Valley Canning Company wasn't put off by a poor first impression.

The Minnesota Valley Canning Company, which is not the catchiest nor most memorable name, was founded in 1903 in Le Sueur, Minnesota. The company used the latest canning technology and had started to ship white creamed corn across the US.

Four years later, it added 'early June peas', and then in 1924, a sweeter, golden, cream-style yellow corn was launched.

In 1925, the company launched yet another new product. This time it was cans of extra-large green peas that had more flavour, and a sweetness and tenderness that early June peas just couldn't match. They decided to call the new product line "Green Giant Great Big Tender Peas".

The new line was reasonably successful, and The Minnesota Valley Canning Company decided to try advertising it in an attempt to further drive sales. They developed a green giant character to star in the advertisement.

The Green Giant's first incarnation was said to have been inspired by *Grimm's Fairy Tales*. He did look rather grim. Scowling, carrying a giant and very heavy pea pod, he wore a scruffy bearskin. He did not look very approachable or friendly, and wasn't even green.

The results of the first campaign, which ran in 1928 were, to say the least, disappointing.

The quality of the product meant that the giant green peas however continued to sell well, in spite rather than because of the advertising. However, The Minnesota Valley Canning Company decided to try again, and gave the account to advertising agency Erwin, Wasey & Co where the assignment for the giant's transformation was given to a young man by the name of Leo Burnett.

Leo straightened the giant's posture, turned his scary scowl into a sunny smile and clothed him in a light, leafy outfit. He also decided to give the giant a new backdrop – a valley of crops that highlighted the Giant's height and stature – The Green Giant Valley.

The advert started to perform and sales accelerated.

Not surprisingly, when Leo Burnett went on to open his own agency in 1935, The Minnesota Valley Canning Company was one of his first clients.

The Burnett agency kept evolving with the giant in the press and poster ads. He became so popular that in 1950,

The Minnesota Valley Canning Company changed its name to Green Giant Co.

But then disaster nearly struck again as the Green Giant was slated to make his television debut.

It was not an easy transition. The agency tried treatments both in animation and with live characters, but the giant did not come across as the friendly protector he was supposed to be. He was once again seen as unappealing and even a little scary.

This problem was solved by creating a set with a tiny valley for the man-sized Giant to preside over. Close-up shots were avoided and the Giant was most often seen off in the distance, protecting the valley and its crops.

He was also re-christened as the Jolly Green Giant and gained his catch phrase "Ho, Ho, Ho!"

When, in 1961, the Green Giant Company introduced frozen vegetables, he appeared with a red scarf to keep him warm. In 1973 he was given an apprentice 'Sprout' whose role was to help the giant tend to the valley and ask all the questions that people might want to ask about the giant and his products.

The Jolly Green Giant is now one of the most recognized advertising icons of all time, *Advertising Age* magazine ranked him as the third most recognizable advertising character of the 20th century, behind only Ronald McDonald and the Marlboro Man.

There is even a 55-ft fiberglass statue of the Jolly Green Giant, which was erected in 1979, presiding over his birthplace in Blue Earth, Minnesota!

And the moral is that literal translations of brand names into icons doesn't always work, sometimes you need some creative licence. How can you adapt your logo to make it more engaging and appealing?

44. CAN A BLUE BOX MAKE A WOMAN'S HEART BEAT FASTER?

It has been said that the mere act of holding a little blue box can make a woman's heart beat faster ...but it has to be a particular shade of blue.

Tiffany Blue is a light medium robin egg blue that has been associated with the world famous company almost since it was founded in 1837, though not actually used until 1845.

Founded by Charles Lewis Tiffany and John B Young in New York City, the brand was originally positioned as a stationery and fancy goods emporium, and operated as Tiffany, Young and Ellis in Lower Manhattan.

The name was shortened to Tiffany & Company in 1853 when Charles Tiffany took control and established the brand's emphasis on jewellery.

At an auction in 1887, Tiffany purchased a third of the French crown jewels, including Empress Eugenie's famous diamond necklace, and earned him the nickname "The King of Diamonds".

The first Tiffany's mail order catalogue was published in 1845 in the United States, and its cover was a distinctive robin egg blue colour. It quickly become known as the "Blue Book" and is still published to this day.

The colour is now protected as a colour trademark in a number of countries and jurisdictions, including the US. It is produced as a private custom colour by Pantone, who gave it the number PMS (Pantone matching System) 1837; a colour that is much better known as "Tiffany Blue". As a trademarked colour, it is not publicly available and is not printed in the Pantone Matching System swatch books.

So, why was that particular shade chosen?

The most often quoted reason is that it was Empress Eugenie's favourite shade. Napoleon III's wife was an early global fashion icon, and helped set the style and trends of the day around the world.

Having seen the immediate appeal of the blue on the catalogue, Charles Lewis Tiffany used it on other promotional materials, including boxes and bags. It was he who mandated that the coveted boxes could only be acquired with a Tiffany purchase.

The *New York Sun* wrote of the box's special appeal in 1906, saying that: "Tiffany has one thing in stock that you cannot buy off him for as much money as you may offer, he will only give it to you. And that is one of his boxes."

And the moral is that brands can own colours and their associations in their customers' minds. What colour would you like to own for your brand, and why?

45. THE STRANGEST BRAND ICON IN THE WORLD

Lions, with their size, huge manes and majestic appearance, are known as "the king of beasts" and have long been used as a symbol of strength, power, leadership and even royalty in art and literature.

It's not surprising, then, that there are many brands that have chosen a lion as their brand icon. They include ING, Peugeot, MGM and the English Premier League, to name just a few.

There is however one brand that uses a dead lion as its logo. Indeed, it's not just a dead lion, but an image of a lion's rotting carcass surrounded by a swarm of bees.

The brand is Lyle's Golden Syrup, one of the oldest brands in Britain.

Lyle's Golden Syrup began life as a by-product from refining sugar cane. However, Abram Lyle discovered that the treacly substance could be turned into a delicious preserve and sweetener for cooking. He developed his production methods and started canning the syrup at Plaistow Wharf in London's Docklands.

Abram Lyle was a deeply religious man, and herein lies the reason for the dead lion.

Chapter 14 of the *Book of Judges* in the *Old Testament* tells the tale of Samson travelling to the land of the Philistines in search of a wife. During the journey he is set upon by a lion, which he kills. When he passes the same spot on his way back he sees the lion is still there, but now it is covered in a swarm of bees and they have made a honeycomb in its carcass.

Samson later turns this vision into a riddle he poses at a wedding: "Out of the eater came forth meat and out of the strong came forth sweetness."

The latter part of the quote "out of the strong came forth sweetness" and the image of the dead lion's carcass complete with the swarm of bees have been the brand's icon since 1904, when they were registered as a trademark.

The lion, the bees and the words remain on the tins today.

And the moral is, the best designs don't just identify, they signify something. Does your brand's design do more than just identify it as your brand?

46. TAKING HIS DAUGHTER'S NAME

You may not know the name Emil Jellinek, but it is highly likely that you know the name of his daughter.

With a love for speed, Jellinek took an early interest in the arrival of the automobile. In 1897, he made the journey to Cannstatt, Germany to visit the Daimler factory and ordered his first Daimler car, a belt-driven vehicle with a six-horse power (hp) two-cylinder engine.

For its time, this car had an impressive top speed of 24km/h, but this was too slow for Jellinek. He ordered two more vehicles, but demanded that they should have a top speed of 40km/h. The two Daimler Phoenix cars he received in response were the world's first road vehicles with four-cylinder engines.

Jellinek was well connected with the world of international finance, and even the aristocracy, so decided to put those contacts to good use. He negotiated a deal with Daimler, and began to promote and sell their cars. In 1899, Daimler-Motoren-Gesellschaft (DMG) supplied Jellinek with ten vehicles; in 1900 the number went up to 29.

Jellinek however continued to demand ever faster and more powerful vehicles for himself, as he had decided he wanted to enter in the new world of automotive race meetings – first and foremost of which was the Nice Week.

Jellinek decided to name his team after his then ten-year-old daughter, and due to his success, it was a name that was soon well known in motoring circles.

In 1900, following on from his success, Jellinek and DMG signed an agreement to produce a new engine which would bear a product name that was a combination of Daimiler and Jellinak's daughter's name. Jellinek ordered 36 of the vehicles with the new engines at a total price of 550,000 marks. This was a huge and very valuable order for the time, but just a few weeks later, he placed a new order for another 36 vehicles.

The first vehicle to be fitted with the new engine, a 35-hp racing car, was delivered to Jellinek by DMG on 22 December 1900. With its low centre of gravity, pressed-steel frame, lightweight high-performance engine and honeycomb radiator, it featured numerous innovations and is still regarded by many as the first modern automobile.

Nice Week in 1901 proved an enormous success and attracted even more publicity for Jellinek and the new cars. DMG quickly launched 12/16-hp and 8/11-hp sister models.

On 23 June 1902, an application was made for DMG to use Jellinek's daughter's name as the trade name, and this was legally registered on the 26 September. His daughter's name, which means 'grace' in Spanish was, of course, Mercédès.

From June 1903, Emil Jellinek obtained permission to call himself Jellinek-Mercedes, and commented that "this is probably the first time a father has taken his daughter's name".

And the moral is, sometimes brand names need a while before they are fully accepted. Have you been too hasty in your judgment of brand names?

47. ANY COLOUR YOU WANT AS LONG AS IT'S BLACK (AND WHITE)

On 29 April 1961, in a small town in Switzerland, a group of eminent people made a commitment to the natural world. They called for urgent worldwide action to stop vast numbers of wild animals being hunted out of existence and habitats destroyed. It began…

"We must save the world's wildlife – An International Declaration. All over the world today vast numbers of fine and harmless wild creatures are losing their lives, or their homes, in an orgy of thoughtless and needless destruction."

The *Morges Manifesto* became the blueprint for one of the world's first 'green' organizations – the World Wildlife Fund (now called simply WWF).

The founders included the respected biologist Julian Huxley. Other signatories came from Belgium, France, Germany, Poland, Sudan, Sweden, Switzerland and the US.

The organization's international secretariat was established in Switzerland in September, and national WWF offices were gradually set up across the world, starting with the UK in November 1961.

Aware of the need for a strong, recognizable identity, they turned naturally to one of their original signatories, the renowned ornithologist and painter Sir Peter Scott, and asked him to come up with recommendations.

Sir Peter was perhaps most famous for painting flocks of geese or ducks flying in the air against a wetland background as the sun was setting or rising. He clearly had the artistic flair to undertake the task.

And while he was happy to take on the brief, he soon learnt there was one small restriction – he couldn't use any colour: the newly formed World Wildlife Fund wanted a design in black and white. The young organization had limited funds, and printing in black and white was considerably cheaper than printing in colour.

Luckily, inspiration came from Chi-Chi: a giant panda that had arrived at the London Zoo in the same year (1961). Sir Peter knew that the big, furry animal with her appealing, black-patched eyes would make an excellent logo.

Sir Peter asked Gerald Watterson, a British environmentalist and artist to produce some initial sketches. Based on these, Sir Peter drew the first logo, and was to say of it:

"We wanted an animal that is beautiful, is endangered, and one loved by many people in the world for its appealing qualities. We also wanted an animal that had an impact in black and white to save money on printing costs."

Though it has been refined (in 1978, 1986 and again in 2000), the simple black and white panda design remains the core logo for WWF, and is now one of the most recognizable brands in the world.

And the moral is, a tight creative brief is often the best brief. Are you doing everything to make sure your brief is clear and concise?

48. MAYBE IT WILL GROW ON ME

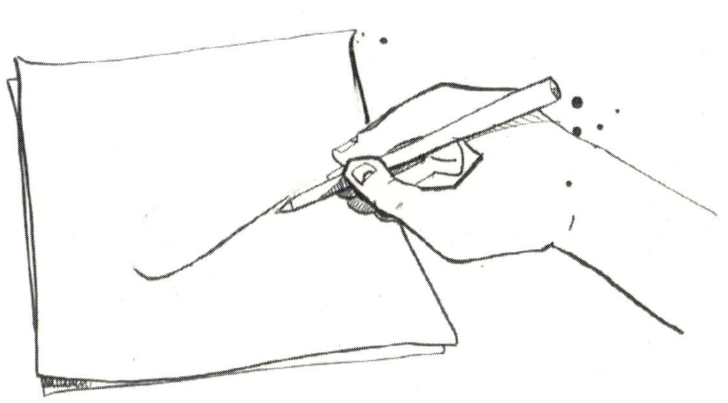

One day in 1971, Carolyn Davidson – a design student at Portland State University (PSU) – was sitting in a college hallway, working on a drawing assignment and bemoaning the fact that she couldn't afford to take an oil-painting class. A young associate professor overheard and asked if she wanted to do some work for him and his fledgling company. He offered to pay her $2 an hour. She accepted.

Phil Knight was that young associate professor. He had taken the job at PSU to supplement the modest income he made running Blue Ribbon Sports, Inc – a fledgling company that served as a West Coast distributor of Japanese-made Tiger brand sneakers in the US.

Davidson's initial work involved making charts and graphs for Knight's meetings with executives visiting from Japan. Knight, however, had bigger plans. He wanted to start selling his own brand of sports shoe. He gave Davidson a new brief. He wanted a logo, or "stripe", for his new brand, Nike – so named after the Greek goddess of victory.

Knight told her it needed to convey motion, but couldn't look like Adidas, Puma or Onitsuka's Tiger logos.

For the next fortnight, Davidson worked on numerous ideas, the best of which she would sketch out by hand on tissue paper and lay over a shoe drawing. In the end, she presented five or six of her designs to Knight and two other Nike executives.

They weren't that impressed. When her initial presentation ended, they asked: "What else you got?"

However, Knight and his team were pressed for time, and it became clear that all three men were at least willing to accept one of Davidson's designs.

Knight summed up his thoughts at the time: "Well, I don't love it, but maybe it will grow on me." Because they needed it so quickly, Davidson didn't even have time to refine her initial design.

In June 1972, the first Nike running shoes bearing Davidson's now famous 'Swoosh' logo were introduced at the US track and field Olympic trials in Eugene, Oregon.

For her services, Davidson billed the company for 17.5 hours of her time …$35.

And the moral is, sometimes brand identities need a while before they are fully accepted. Have you been too hasty in your judgment of brand identities?

Footnote: Carolyn Davidson graduated from PSU in 1971 with a Bachelor's in graphic design. She continued to work for Nike, designing ads, brochures, posters and catalogues. As the company grew exponentially there came a point late in 1975 when it became clear that her one-person design shop was too small to handle all of Nike's advertising and design needs. Nike and Davidson agreed it was time for a full-service ad agency. She opted to split her time homemaking and doing some freelance design work.

In 1983, three years after it went public, the executives at Nike surprised her with a party. In addition, they presented her with a gold ring in the shape of her Swoosh, complete with a small diamond. They also gave her a certificate of appreciation and 500 shares of stock.

Of that gift, Davidson says: "It was something rather special for Phil to do, because I originally billed him and he paid that invoice." She has never sold her shares, which are said to be worth between $0.5-1 million today.

49. THE BANKER, THE STATIONER AND THE ENGINEER

What happens when a banker, an engineer and a stationer meet?

Well, if it's in the first few years of the 20th century in Hamburg, then a truly special brand is created.

Stationer Claus-Johannes Voss, banker Alfred Nehemias and engineer August Eberstein came together in 1906 and founded the Simplo Filler Pen company. They started producing up-market pens in the Schanzen district of Hamburg.

Their first model was the Rouge et Noir. But this was swiftly followed in 1910 by a pen that later gave its name to the company, Montblanc. It promised: "No blots on your Sunday dress."

The story goes that the idea for the name came during a card game, when a relative of one of the founders drew an analogy between the new pen – which aimed to become the pinnacle of writing instruments – and Mont Blanc, the majestic and highest peak in the nearby Alps. The partners loved the idea and the name was adopted. And in keeping with the analogy, the pen was given a white tip.

The name stuck, but in 1913 the white tip design evolved into a white star with six rounded points that tops every Montblanc pen.

Both designs are now registered trademarks.

There is, however, still some debate as to exactly what the new logo is supposed to represent. Some say it is a snowflake, others say it is simply a depiction of a mountain top, while in the book *Montblanc in Denmark 1914-1992 – The Untold Story*, authors Holten and Lund put the case for a star.

They say: "It is no coincidence that the Montblanc headquarters from 1908 were situated in the Hamburg borough 'Sternschanze'. The German word stern means star in English. Sternschanze means starfortification – a fortification with the shape of a star."

Shops and restaurants in the area still use a white star as symbol of the district.

The mountain theme is further reinforced by the number 4810, Mont Blanc's height in metres, which was engraved on the nib of the brand's leading model the Meisterstück (or Masterpiece in English) for the first time in 1929. It is still a recurring theme in the brand's communications today.

And the moral is, a brand identity can be expressed in many forms across different media. How could you further develop your brand's communication equities?

50. NO ORDINARY WHISKY, NO ORDINARY NAME

Monkey Shoulder is not your ordinary whisky.

It is described as tasting like "riding bareback on the wild moors of Scotland with a flame-haired maiden on Christmas morning", or "007 wearing a tuxedo wetsuit". (I must admit the first description had me desperately wanting to try it, while the second nearly put me off).

Launched in 2005, it was the idea of William Grant & Sons' malt master at the time, David Stewart. He wanted to create the first 'triple' malt whisky. He combined three different Speyside Single Malts – Glenfiddich, Balvenie and Kininvie – to delicious effect.

The name, which sounds exotic, has mundane origins.

Monkey shoulder is slang for a physical condition that

commonly afflicted maltmen in the past, who worked long shifts, turning the barley manually using large wooden shovels. The arduous work had a tendency to cause their lead arm to hang down a bit like a monkey's and people would refer to it as monkey shoulder.

William Grant, which owns and produces the brand, is proud to say its maltmen still turn the barley manually, but shifts are shorter and less arduous so monkey shoulder is no longer a problem.

The name is meant as an affectionate tribute "to honour the hard graft of all maltmen past and present".

And the moral is that your product history can be an inspiration for a new brand name. Can you look back to find a name for the future?

MARKETING STRATEGY

You know what you want to do, but how are you going to actually do it?

Who should you target, and why?

How can you go about getting them to try your brand?

It's great to have a vision of where you want to go, but you need the plans and actions that will get you there. What is your strategy, and how are you going to deliver it? If you can't out-spend the competition, can you out-think it?

Can you segment a market to your advantage? Should you zig while everyone else is zagging? Can you see an opportunity where others only see problems? Are you building a brand or starting a revolution?

These stories may allow you to steal your next strategy with pride.

51. THE LADDER TO SUCCESS

"I'm going to democratize the automobile," Henry Ford said in 1909. "When I'm through, everybody will be able to afford one, and about everybody will have one."

Using the highly cost-effective assembly-line method to produce cars, he had developed the Model T, with which his Ford Motor Car Company took control of the market. His vision was built on economies of scale, and his focus on making just one model: "You can have any colour you like as long as it's black."

It was this that gave Ford the ability to grow and develop in the early market. This also created the opportunity that Alfred Sloan and General Motor needed to exploit and overtake Ford to become market leaders.

Sloan was born in New Haven, Connecticut, and studied electrical engineering at the Massachusetts Institute of Technology (MIT).

He went on to become president and owner of Hyatt Roller Bearing, a company that made roller and ball bearings. It started to supply early automotive companies like Oldsmobile with the ball bearing they needed.

Then, in 1916, on the back of the rapidly expanding car market, Hyatt merged with a number of other companies to become the United Motors Company, which in turn soon became part of General Motors Corporation. Sloan became vice-president of GM, then president in 1923, and finally in 1937, chairman of the board.

Sloan's approach to business management demonstrated a flair for marketing and consumer insight.

He realized that consumer tastes changed and evolved, and that not everyone's taste was the same. While a basic cheap and functional car suited many, it didn't suit everyone – especially the more affluent customers who wanted more power, more style and status.

So he came up with a concept he called "a car for every purse and purpose". The idea was to have five distinctive brands that did not compete with each other (from the lowest costing car to the most expensive). These were Chevrolet, Pontiac, Oldsmobile, Buick and Cadillac. Each offered choice and variety to different groups of customers. Customers could, as their income grew, move from brand to brand, moving up what Sloan called "the ladder of success".

Sloan introduced a five-way segmentation into the market.

To meet the need for changing tastes, and to encourage people to come back and buy another car, he introduced frequent styling changes in his models. So if you wanted to keep up with the latest trends, you needed to buy a new car. It is often labelled as the introduction of "planned obsolescence". Though, in reality, he was mirroring what was going on in other industries, like fashion.

These changes – along with Ford's resistance to change – worked, and GM overtook Ford sales by the early 1930s, a position it was to retain for the next 70 years.

Sloan's ladder of success was to prove a ladder to success for GM.

And the moral is that balancing economies of production with a selectively tailored offer is at the heart of marketing segmentation. How can you segment your market to your advantage?

52. WHEN LESS WAS MORE

"Silicon Valley's paragon of dysfunctional management and fumbled techno-dreams, is back in crisis mode, scrambling lugubriously in slow motion to deal with imploding sales, a floundering technology strategy, and a haemorrhaging brand name," so wrote *Fortune* magazine in 1996 about none other than Apple.

During the final quarter of 1996, Apple's sales plummeted by 30% and the brand was on the brink of failure. Luckily, riding to the rescue came the prodigal son – Steve Jobs, who returned to Apple in 1997, the company he co-founded more than two decades earlier.

A partnership deal with Microsoft injected $150 million into Apple and created a lifeline, but didn't solve the underlying problems.

Reviewing the business, Jobs was amazed to find the sheer number of different products being produced. Apple was producing multiple versions of the same product, each with minor but expensive little twists, to satisfy requests from retailers – they were selling a dozen different versions of the Macintosh computer.

To test his theory that many of these were completely unnecessary, he asked his team of top managers: "Which ones do I tell my friends to buy?"

No-one could give him a simple answer, but Jobs had a simple answer to the problem.

He set about reducing the number of Apple products by 70%. Among the products to go was the Newton digital personal assistant. Another unfortunate consequence was a reduction in the workforce by approximately 3,000 employees.

"Deciding what not to do is as important as deciding what to do," Jobs said in a later interview. "It's true for companies, and it's true for products."

Jobs announced a strategy, which for computing meant focusing on only four products: two for professionals – the Power Macintosh G3 desktop and the PowerBook G3 portable computer; and two for consumers – the iMac desktop and iBook portable computer.

The other focus was a selected number of innovations.

The turn-around wasn't instantaneous. At the end of Jobs' first fiscal year back, Apple lost just over a $1billion and was in his own words "90 days from being insolvent".

One year later, however, the company turned a $309 million profit.

And the moral is (as Steve Jobs said), deciding what not to do is as important as deciding what to do. What should you be saying 'NO' to?

53. A STELLAR APPROACH TO SELLING TYRES

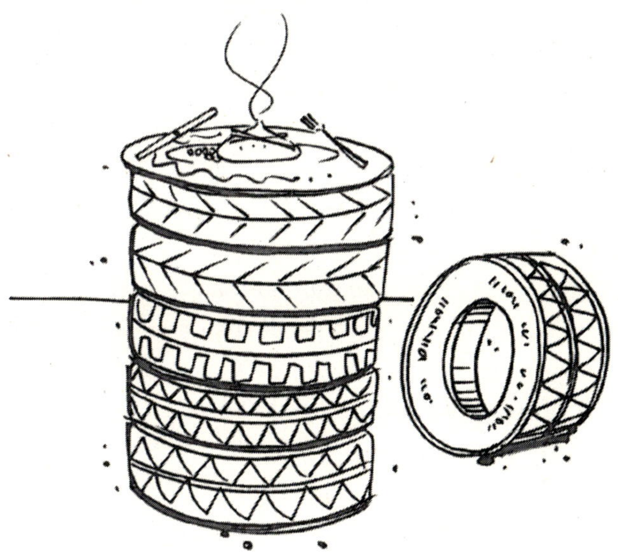

Round black and rubbery isn't something you would necessarily associate with food unless you have ever been served burnt squid. But when you add the word 'Michelin', the connection is more obvious.

The origins of the now famous *Michelin Guide* and its star-rating system are similarly obscure. Those origins can be traced back to 1900, a time when there were only a few thousand cars on the road in France. Brothers André and Édouard Michelin were looking for clever new ways to promote the sale of their tyres, and decided upon the notion of a travellers' guide – *The Michelin Guide*. Their thinking was that if people travelled more, they would wear down their tyres and so have to buy new ones.

The original guides were given away free of charge, and contained useful information for motorists, including maps, instructions for repairing and changing tyres, and lists of car mechanics, hotels and petrol stations. In 1904, the brothers published a similar guide to Belgium, and in subsequent years guides for other European countries followed.

Not surprisingly, publication was stopped during world war I. And when printing resumed after the war, the brothers were soon to review their policy of giving them away free.

When visiting a tyre merchant one day, André Michelin saw a pile of copies being used to prop up a workbench, and decided that perhaps the old adage of "man only truly respects what he pays for" was correct after all.

The brothers decided to start charging for the guide, but they took the opportunity to make some changes to it, listing restaurants, and abandoning advertisements in the guide.

The popularity, and indeed use, of the new restaurant section encouraged the brothers to expand it, and they recruited a special team of inspectors to visit and review the restaurants. These early Michelin inspectors were instructed to carefully maintain their anonymity ensuring the independence of the review.

In 1926, the guide awarded its first stars for fine dining. Initially there was only one tier – either you got a star, or you didn't.

It wasn't until 1931 that the hierarchy of one, two and three stars was introduced, and another five years before the criteria for the different levels was published:

One star: "A very good restaurant in its category – worth stopping" ("*Une très bonne table dans sa catégorie*")

Two stars: "Excellent cooking, worth a detour" ("*Table excellente, mérite un détour*")

Three stars: "Exceptional cuisine, worth a special journey" ("*Une des meilleures tables, vaut le voyage*").

And the moral is that promotional items can add value in their own right. Can you monetize any of your promotional items?

Footnote: During world war II publication was again suspended, but in 1944, at the request of the Allied Forces, the 1939 guide to France was specially reprinted for military use: its maps were judged the best and most up-to-date available to the invading armies. Publication of the annual guide resumed on 16 May 1945, a week after VE Day.

54. A BIRD IN THE AIR IS WORTH A BOOK IN THE HAND

BANG!
BANG!
"Damn!"

He had missed the shot and the plover flew off to safety.

It was November 1951 and Sir Hugh Beaver, a keen shot and the then MD of Guinness Breweries, was with a shooting party in North Slob, on the River Slaney in County Wexford, Ireland.

Disappointed at missing, Sir Hugh consoled himself with the fact that the golden plover is the fastest game bird in Europe. At least, that is what he thought.

A lively debate was soon raging among various members of the party: was the plover actually the fastest game bird, or was it the red grouse? The argument continued all the way back to Castlebridge House where the shooting party was staying.

Unfortunately, despite an exhaustive search, none of the reference books in the library could confirm who was right.

Sir Hugh could have been frustrated – no bird and now no answer, but looking for positives in the negatives, he realized that here was an opportunity. If he and his shooting party were annoyed by this unresolved question, how many more debates were still raging in the pubs and clubs up and down the land?

Could Guinness, which was available and drunk in places where so many of these arguments occurred, become the provider of definitive answers?

And so the notion for *The Guinness Book of Records* was born (and wasn't shot down!).

And the moral is, you never know when a business opportunity will arise. Are your ears and eyes open to opportunity 24/7?

Footnote: Sir Hugh was in fact correct; the golden plover is the fastest game bird in Europe.

55. WAKE UP AND (DON'T) SMELL THE COFFEE

It is often said that you should never go back. But Howard Schultz had the courage to return to the helm of the brand he had helped create.

In 2000, Schultz stepped down as CEO of Starbucks and relinquished daily control of the company, assuming the role of chairman.

Seven years later, he was worried. While he recognized that he had been party to some of the changes that now so concerned him, he felt he couldn't stand by and do nothing. He was later to observe in his book *Onward*, that "the damage was slow and quiet, incremental, like a single loose thread that unravels a sweater inch by inch".

So he wrote his now (in)famous letter to Jim Donald, the then CEO, entitled, "The commoditization of the Starbucks experience".

In it he said: "Over the past ten years, in order to achieve the growth, development, and scale necessary to go from less than 1,000 stores to 13,000 stores and beyond, we have had to make a series of decisions that, in retrospect, have led to the watering down of the Starbucks experience, and, what some might call the commoditization of our brand."

Schultz had woken up and smelt the coffee; or rather had woken up because he couldn't smell the coffee anymore. He decried the loss of theatre and romance in the stores, and in particular the move to using bagged coffee rather than freshly ground, which had led to the "loss of aroma – perhaps the most powerful non-verbal signal we had in our stores".

He went on to write that he believed the stores "no longer have the soul of the past, and reflect a chain of stores vs the warm feeling of a neighbourhood store. Some people even call our stores sterile, cookie cutter, no longer reflecting the passion our partners feel about our coffee".

He recognized that the all-out pursuit of growth as a strategy had become addictive. As he later said in an interview in *McKinsey Quarterly*: "Growth should not be – and is not – a strategy; it's a tactic. The primary lesson I've learned over the years is that growth and success can cover up a lot of mistakes."

So in 2008, in the midst of the recession and during a period of decline, Schultz returned to the CEO post and started to put right some of those mistakes. In the next couple of years, he led a dramatic turn-around of the business and the brand.

His first act, in February 2008, was to invite employees to email him directly, letting him know what they thought. He immediately received 5,000 emails.

In the 2009 financial year, he set out to cut over $500 million worth of costs. He cut deeply and quickly, shedding around 800 stores in the US, hundreds more in its international networks, and losing over 7% of his workforce. Annual revenue likewise fell.

However, some of his actions demonstrated his on-going belief in the values of the brand. He refused to cut health care for thousands of part-time baristas, despite pressure from outsiders who could see more savings.

He also committed to doubling its annual purchase of fair-trade certified coffee to 40 million lbs in 2009.

His next job was to bring the romance back to the brand and take Starbucks back to its roots of providing great coffee. Starbucks developed and rolled out a new flexible design for all of its stores. Schultz re-instated the selling coffee paraphernalia in store, and brought back freshly roasted coffee. He insisted baristas grind the beans in the stores, and any coffee that had been sitting for more than 30 minutes had to be thrown away.

But his most symbolic move was made in February 2008, which was to close all 7,100 US stores for three-and-a-half hours to re-train baristas. It is estimated that this alone cost Starbucks $6m.

He also extended the brand into one place people weren't often consuming Starbucks, their homes, by overseeing the creation of the instant coffee brand called VIA. Despite some early scepticism, the range has proved a success.

Starbucks' annual revenue in 2012 was $14bn, with some 150,000 employees around the world. More importantly, when Howard Schultz goes to bed at night, he now knows that the next morning he will wake up and smell the coffee, freshly roasted coffee.

And the moral is, short term growth isn't everything. Are you staying true to your brand's core values?

56. THE SALESMAN IN BASKETBALL'S HALL OF FAME

Long before Michael Jordan and Nike created their successful partnership, another brand, which is coincidently now owned by Nike, created an even more successful partnership with a basketball player.

It is in fact the best-selling basketball shoe of all time and one that around 60% of all Americans own, or have owned in the past.

The brand is Converse, the star was Charles H Taylor (better known as Chuck), and the sneakers in question were the Converse All Star "Chuck Taylor" Basketball Shoes.

Founded by Marquis Mills Converse in 1908, the Converse Rubber Corporation began life not as a sports shoe manufacturer, but instead making galoshes and other work-related rubber shoes on a seasonal basis.

After a few years, the company decided to expand with the aim of keeping its work force employed all year round. It identified the growing popularity of basketball as an opportunity and decided to develop a rubber-soled shoe that people could wear while playing the game. The result went into production in 1917. It was the original All Star. It consisted of a very thick rubber sole, and an ankle covering canvas (or sometimes leather) top.

Sales, unlike the best basketball players, were slow. But all that started to change in 1921.

The driving force was Chuck Taylor.

Taylor was a high-school basketball player at Columbus High School and, on discovering them in 1917, he started wearing Converse shoes. In 1921, Taylor went to the Converse Shoes Chicago sales offices in search of a job, where SR "Bob" Pletz, an avid sportsman, recognized him and immediately hired him.

Taylor proved to be not only an effective salesman, but also an on-going source of ideas that would help improve the brand – both the product and its marketing. As a player, he knew what other players wanted so started making suggestions on how to change the design of the shoe to provide enhanced flexibility and support. The suggestions also included a patch to protect the ankle, onto which the star logo was added.

In 1922, Taylor launched the Converse Basketball Yearbook, in which the best players, trainers, teams, and the greatest moments of the sport were commemorated. It proved to be good publicity, and in 1928 it was extended.

The "Basketball Clinic" was, however, his main interest and the means he used for showcasing Converse All Stars.

The first one was held at North Carolina State University in 1922. His next "demonstration", as he would sometimes describe it, was for Fielding Yost at the University of Michigan, followed by one at Columbia. Chuck continued to travel the country, in his distinctive white Cadillac, holding his clinics for the next 30 years. Steve Stone, a former Converse president, reflecting on their success said: "Chuck's gimmick was to go to a small town, romance the coach, and put on a clinic. He would teach basketball and work with the local sporting goods dealer, but without encroaching on the coach's own system."

In 1932, in recognition of his success, Chuck Taylor's signature was added to the patch, and the shoe was renamed the Chuck Taylor All Stars.

He designed the white high top model for the 1936 Olympics, with its patriotic red and blue trim.

Taylor received a salary from Converse and, it must be said, a generous expense account – which he is understood to have used freely. But he received no commission for any of the 800-million-plus pairs of Chuck Taylor shoes that have now been sold.

Taylor made other contributions to the sport of basketball, including in 1935 the invention of the "stitchless" basketball that was easier to control.

Thanks to his tireless efforts promoting the sport, and his shoes, Taylor was often called the "ambassador to basketball", and in 1968, Charles H 'Chuck' Taylor was inducted into the Basketball Hall of Fame.

He died in 1969, but his shoes live on.

And the moral is, the best celebrity endorsements are much more than advocacy. Are you using any celebrity endorsements you have to maximum mutual effect?

57. A VALENTINE'S ROMANCE – WHEN KEN MET BARBIE

They first met on a film set, where they appeared together in a TV commercial.

The attraction was instant. They became one of the world's most famous couples.

Then, on Valentine's Day 2004, she announced they were no longer a couple.

She was seen out and about, on the town. He faded from view.

They met again on another film set in 2010. The film was a smash and his star was on the rise again.

Determined to win her back, he started an all-out campaign.

Then on Valentine's Day 2011, the news broke, they were officially an item again.

Just another celebrity love match?

Not quite, this is the true 'toy' story of how Ken met Barbie, how Ken lost Barbie and how he won her back.

"And then it happened – she met Ken, and somehow she just knew they'd be going together" so went the voice-over in the TV commercial showing that auspicious first meeting in 1961.

It was a long and lasting romance. Though never officially married, they were together for an amazing 43 years. Countless outfits and various makeovers came and went, but on Valentine's Day in 2004, they parted. Russell Arons, Mattel's then vice president of marketing, announced: "Like other celebrity couples, their Hollywood romance has come to an end." But he added, the two "will remain friends".

The newly single Barbie soon had a new companion, Blaine, an Australian surfer.

But Ken never really gave up on Barbie. In 2006, with a makeover – courtesy of Hollywood stylist Phillip Bloch – he reappeared on the scene, but to little effect. Then in 2009, to help Barbie celebrate her 50th anniversary, he made a surprise appearance on the runway at her first New York Fashion Week show.

The party was a great success for Barbie, but did little for Ken's plan to woo her back. However, his appearance caught the eye of the people at Pixar, and the following year Pixar brought them back together in front of the cameras for Toy Story 3.

The reunion 'convinced' Ken it was worth one last try at rekindling the romance, and in a world that had changed so dramatically since they first met all those years ago, he launched a multimedia campaign.

'He' bought posters around New York and Los Angeles on which he 'Ken-fessed' his love: "Barbie, you are the only doll for me." And: "Barbie, we may be plastic but our love is real."

He launched a Facebook page and got a Twitter account "making him real for consumers rather than just an accessory", according to Lauren Bruksch, Mattel's marketing director for Barbie and girls.

Mattel partnered with Match.com, and together they created a video showing Ken searching for new love interests, only to find that his perfect match was still Barbie.

Millions of people watched their on-line flirting. A "Love-O-Meter" was created on BarbieandKen.com where people were asked to say whether Barbie should take him back or not. Over 500,000 fans voted, and they overwhelmingly supported a make-up.

Finally, Barbie succumbed, and on Valentine's Day 2011 it was announced that they were officially back together.

Thoroughly modern and new-media savvy Barbie told TODAYshow.com: "I'm in awe of the lengths Ken went to profess his love, he knows how to sweep a doll off her feet!"

It was a great PR coup for Barbie, Ken and their manufacturer Mattel.

And the moral is, creating content is a powerful means of building engagement with your brand. Are you creating the content around your brand?

58. DON'T MENTION THE. . .LADY DAYS

Even 100 years on, it is hard to imagine the true scale of death and injury caused by World War I. During the heaviest periods of fighting, soldiers were getting wounded in such large numbers that the medics often ran out of bandages.

To try and help overcome this problem, Kimberly-Clark – a leading manufacturer of mostly paper-based personal care products – offered the army a new product of theirs: "Cellucotton" – a highly absorbent fluffy paper wadding. Cellucotton could be used for filters in gas masks, stuffing for emergency jackets, but most importantly for pads and bandages.

Commendably, Kimberly-Clark decided they'd sell Cellucotton to the War Department and Red Cross at no profit.

However, it was not long after their arrival at the battlefields that a new and completely unexpected use was found for some of the bandages. The female nurses and the nuns tending the wounded started using them for their "Lady Days" (as periods were referred to then). The new bandages worked much better, and were more hygienic, than the pieces of rags which were being used.

When Armistice day arrived and the war was finally over, Kimberly-Clark found it had partially filled orders for 750,000 lbs of Cellucotton, and in another altruistic act Kimberly-Clark allowed these orders to be cancelled without penalty. It left the company with a huge surplus. Worse still, the Army also had a large surplus of Cellucotton – and they began selling it to civilian hospitals at a ridiculously low price, instantaneously killing the market for Kimberley-Clark.

Kimberley-Clark had to try and find a new use for the product, and fast.

Luckily, word had reached them about their alternative use. They decided to try to market them to women as feminine hygiene pads.

The rechristened Cellunaps were positioned to retailers as the first disposable sanitary napkin. Retailers, while seeing the potential, were worried about public sensitivity and insisted they were not suitable for public display, so must stay behind the druggists' counter.

Sales did not go well. Women were unhappy asking the mostly male assistants for them over the counter.

Kimberley Clark decided on a new approach. They changed the name to KOTEX, a meaningless worger (word merger) of c[K]Otton-like TEXture that would hopefully not reveal anything in a crowded drugstore. The second, and perhaps crucial, change was the introduction of counter displays so that women could buy their Kotex without talking to the clerk.

As counter and shelf displays grew, so did sales and the brand.

And the moral is, it is easy to forget how important being on display – mental availability – is. What are you doing to maximize your mental availability?

Footnote: As Kotex sales began to grow, letters started to pour in to the company, mostly favourable. But many were from women who wanted to know more about their bodies and the menstrual process. As a result, Kimberly-Clark built its Education Division and began mailing out information packs, including a pamphlet called 'Marjorie May's 12th Birthday', which was initially banned in some states for being too sexually explicit.

Later, they were to work with the Disney Company to create a movie called 'The Story of Menstruation', which would be shown in schools and was seen by over 70 million schoolchildren – a most-unlikely most-watched movie from the Disney catalogue.

59. THE (W)HOLE STORY?

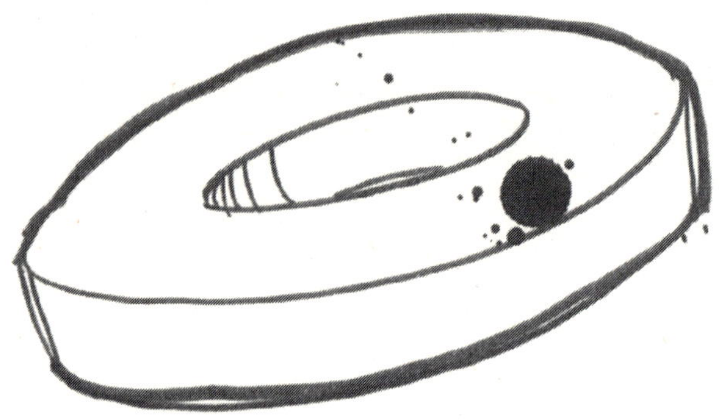

Clarence Crane had a problem. He was a chocolate maker – and a good one, but every summer his business fell away. It was the early 20th century, and he found it hard to transport his chocolate without it melting during the hot summer months in Garrettsville, Ohio.

He decided to try and develop some 'summer candy', and fixed on the idea of peppermint sweets. Now, at that time most of the mints available came from Europe, and they were square in shape. However, one day when buying bottles of flavouring in a drug store, he noticed a pharmacist using a pill-making machine. It was operated by hand and made round, flat pills.

Crane had an idea: he could use the machine to make his mints. Then he had what was perhaps an even more inspired thought: he decided to punch a small hole in the middle of each one.

This distinctive shape led not only to a memorable advertising line: "The candy with the hole", but also gave the brand its name – Crane's Peppermint LifeSavers. Ring-shaped, predominately white life-preservers were increasingly being used on ships, and the similarity was apparent to all immediately. Crane registered the trademark.

In 1913, however, Crane made a poor decision and sold the recipe for LifeSavers to Edward John Noble for only $2,900.

Noble founded his own company The LifeSavers and Candy Company in 1913, and started selling his Pep-O-Mint LifeSavers.

His first move was to try and improve product quality, so replaced the cardboard rolls used as packaging with tin-foil wrappers to keep the mints fresh. This process was done by hand until 1919 when machinery was developed by Edward's brother, Robert, which streamlined the process.

Ahead of their time, the brothers recognized the power of what we today call 'impulse purchasing', and encouraged restaurants, saloons, cigar shops and grocers to have LifeSavers displays next to their cash registers.

Again, with great insight and an intuitive understanding of what today we call 'behavioural economics', they also trained the owners of these establishments to always give customers a nickel in their change. LifeSavers cost a nickel at the time, and this clever move both encouraged and facilitated their easy purchase.

The third strand of their ambitious growth plan was to introduce a variety of different flavours. By 1919, six other flavours – Wint-O-Green, Cl-O-ve, Lic-O-Riche, Cinn-O-Mon, Vi-O-Let and Choc-O-Late had been developed.

Another unexpected factor came into play in 1919, which was to boost sales even further. The 1919 approval of the 18th Amendment, the National Prohibition Act, banned the sale of alcohol in the United States. Alcohol went underground, and the foresight of placing breath freshening Pep-O-Mint LifeSavers near cash-registers gave the brand its unexpected lift as they became a means of concealing consumption of illicit booze.

And the moral is, if you have a seasonal product, it is worth exploring opportunities across the year. How can you extend the usage of your brand?

Footnotes: There is an urban legend that Crane actually put the hole in the candies to prevent children from choking, due to his own child having choked on a hard candy, and that this was the reason they were called 'life-savers'. However, records suggest that this is not true.

Polo, like Lifesavers, is a brand of sweets whose defining feature is the hole in the middle. They are extremely popular in the UK where many people believe they were the original mint with a hole. However, this isn't true. The first was manufactured in the United Kingdom in 1948 by employee John Bargewell at the Rowntree's Factory. The name 'Polo' is reportedly from the word 'Polar' and is to symbolize the cool and fresh feeling one gets from sucking a Polo.

60. THE ORIGINAL INCREDIBLES

The world's largest passenger aircraft was built with a budget that could have brought down the company; no wonder the 50,000 employees who worked on the project were dubbed "The Incredibles".

With rising prosperity and the launch of the first successful jet passenger plane in 1958 – the Boeing 707 – air travel grew exponentially in the early 1960s. Juan Trippe, then president of Pan American Airlines, recognized this rapidly growing demand and asked Boeing to develop a new plane that could carry 400 passengers – twice the capacity of a 707. He wanted the extra space and he wanted it now!

Luckily for him his timing was perfect; Boeing had just been working on a design for a supersize plane as part of the US Air Force's C-5 military mega-lifter competition. Although Boeing lost out to Lockheed, it had started to gain the technology and design experience that would allow it to produce the plane Trippe wanted.

Boeing launched a massive fast-track programme to design and build what was to become the 747.

That original design had included a full-length double-deck fuselage with eight-across seating and two aisles on the lower deck, and seven-across seating and two aisles on the upper deck. Concerns about evacuation routes and the limited cargo-carrying capability meant it was dropped in favour of a wider single deck design – a two-aisle ten-abreast main cabin layout which was the world's first "wide-body" plane.

A shortened upper deck was retained, which included the cockpit and allowed for a special freight-loading door to be included in the nose cone – the result was a distinctive bulge. For a while, Boeing wasn't sure what to do with the additional space in the pod behind the cockpit, until someone suggested it could be a lounge area with no permanent seating.

One of the principal technologies that enabled an aircraft as large as the 747 to be created was the development of the high-bypass turbofan engine. This new and revolutionary engine technology was thought to be capable of delivering double the power of the earlier turbojets while consuming a third less fuel.

General Electric had pioneered the concept, but was committed to developing the engine for the Air Force and Lockheed C-5 Galaxy. Luckily for Boeing, Pratt & Whitney was also working on the same technology, and together they developed the JT9D high-bypass turbofans which were more powerful, more fuel-efficient, and quieter than any previous commercial jet engines.

They would need to be, as the new plane was nearly as long as a football field, with a tail that was six stories high and had a take-off weight that was almost triple that of the first 707.

In all, Boeing's up-front investment in the 747 totalled more than $1 billion. If the airplane failed, it would have taken the company down with it.

Many analysts at the time were quick to predict disaster – it would be too big to fly, would cause catastrophic crashes, crumpled runways, and gridlocked passenger terminals.

They must have thought they were right when the first 747 rolled out on 30 September 1968 was immediately hit by problems. However, 'The Incredibles' redoubled their efforts, and by December 1969 the plane was certified as airworthy.

Pan Am began their 747 service in 1970 and although the first flight was seven hours late due to engine trouble the 747 soon silenced the critics by fitting almost seamlessly into the world's airport and terminal systems.

By the end of 2005, 1,365 747s had been delivered to 80 different customers and had flown 3.5 billion passengers, the equivalent of more than half the world's population. Along the way, the 747 was rechristened the Jumbo – a nickname that showed how quickly it won the public's affection.

And the moral is, the best brands transfer learning across their business units. What learning should you be sharing further?

61. ZIGGING WHEN THE WORLD WAS ZAGGING

Founded by Reid Hoffman, Allen Blue, Konstantin Guericke, Eric Ly, and Jean-Luc Vaillant on 5 May 2003, LinkedIn has gone on to have the sort of success so many start-ups can only dream about.

Looking back, 2003 was the heyday of services like Friendster and MySpace, so the creation of yet another social network didn't really seem to be a sensible option.

However, as Guericke was later to tell Bloomberg *Businessweek*, LinkedIn set out with a view to be different from the traditional social and youth-orientated networks. Instead of appealing to teenagers and young adults who wanted to share their updates with the world, they decided to go after an older generation who were into professional development and looking for a new way of doing business.

"We're here to build a business, not to create something cool. MySpace and Facebook have done really well. And I think they can monetize what they have built, probably by adding in more e-commerce. But I think the opportunity on the business side is ultimately larger."

Their business idea was built on the insight that: "People who have been working for at least ten years have a network. It doesn't come from networking; it just comes automatically, from going to work. But people tend to lose touch."

Guericke believed that: "Those networks are valuable. I see business as a Darwinian enterprise. People tend to hire and make other business decisions by drawing on these personal networks. Is a job candidate honest or hard-working? You can't tell from a resume or even from an interview. That's why people fall back on trusted relationships."

This point of difference was what gave the company confidence, even in what Hoffman remembers as the 'dot-com winter' following the bursting of the 'dot-com bubble' in 2000. He says that consumer internet ventures were looked upon with scepticism, so it was crucially important for new ventures to distinguish themselves from everyone else.

According to Chris Saccheri, formerly LinkedIn's director of web development, in the early days, user adoption was rather slow. In the first week, the service had 2,500 users, which grew to 6,000 after the first month. Within six months, there were still only 37,000 users compared to Friendster, which had grown to three million users within three months of going live.

Two years after launching, LinkedIn had more than 1.7 million professionals signed up and was ready to show that those networks were valuable, not only to the professional who could now remain in touch, but as a source of income for the business.

Their first move was the launch of LinkedIn Jobs – combining online job listings with its recommendation engine. Building on its ability to let hiring managers assess a candidate's viability through their relationships, references, and reputation utilizing its LinkedInsight feature, it differentiated itself from competitors like Monster, HotJobs, and CareerBuilder.

Since then, other services have followed like subscription programmes, sponsored updates and service and premium accounts.

LinkedIn reached profitability in March 2006.

In June 2013, just over ten years after launch, LinkedIn reported more than 259 million acquired users in more than 200 countries and territories, with nearly $325 million in quarterly revenue.

And the moral is that there are opportunities in being the same but different. How can you find a new angle in an existing market space?

62. PAMELA ANDERSON, THE SHERMAN TANK AND THE FAILED INVASION OF AMERICA

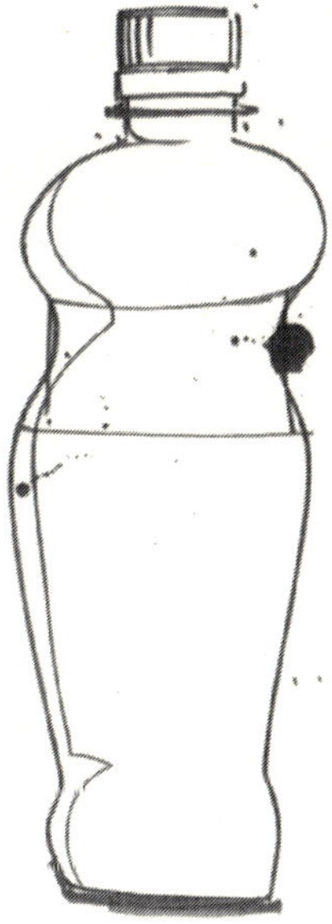

Since Richard Branson started his first business in 1966, the Virgin name has been applied to close to 100 different companies. Everything from railways to make-up, from vodka to video. Some have been incredibly successful, like Virgin Records, Virgin Atlantic and Virgin Media. Some haven't. In fact, some have been incredibly unsuccessful, sinking without trace. This is the story of one of the biggest failures.

Virgin Cola was set up during the early 1990s in conjunction with Cott, a Canadian company that specializes in bottling own-label drinks. Cott was looking for a major brand that could have global appeal, and thought it had found the perfect match.

Virgin, too, had high hopes for the brand. And, having secured a distribution deal with Tesco in 1994, Virgin Cola got off to a flying start.

"The business that looked like it was going to become the number one business in the world was Virgin Cola. We decided to take on the might of Coca Cola. We had a great brand. We had a great product. It tasted better than Coke. We launched it in the UK, we were outselling Coke, outselling Pepsi, and for one wonderful year we had dreams of Virgin Cola being the brand on everybody's lips when they wanted on buy a soft drink," Branson recalls.

However, after that first year, things got a lot tougher. Coke went on the attack increasing its marketing spend and doing widespread promotions which reduced any price advantage Virgin offered. Soon Virgin Cola started to lose share, and with it shelf space, and even distribution.

Virgin tried to respond. In 1996 it decided anything Coke could do they could do better. So they launched "The Pammy".

The Pammy was a specially designed 500ml bottle, with a curvaceously contoured body designed to resemble Pamela Anderson – the *Baywatch* actress who was at the height of her popularity in the UK. It was both a homage to and a pastiche of the classic Coke bottle, which is often known as the Mae West (after the famous 1930s actress).

The impact was limited and the brand continued to decline.

Increasingly desperate, Branson decided if Virgin couldn't beat Coke in the UK, why not take the fight to Coke's homeland, the US. In 1998, Virgin Cola was launched into the US market in spectacular style. Branson rode a vintage Sherman tank through New York's Times Square, taking aim at a huge Coca-Cola billboard. He then placed a 40-foot Virgin Cola billboard right above the Times Square Virgin Megastore.

Virgin Drinks USA subsequently agreed distribution channels with US retailers, such as Target, but success was again limited and the company closed in April 2001, having managed to establish no more than a 0.5% volume share of the market.

In 2002, a vanilla cola called Virgin Vanilla was launched in the UK, ahead of the launch of a similar product from rival Coca-Cola.

In 2007, Silver Spring acquired the UK licence. However, in 2012 that company fell into administration and ceased production. No company acquired the UK Virgin Cola licence in its place.

But Branson has learnt to take failure in his stride.

"My mother drummed into me from an early age that I should not spend much time regretting the past. I try to bring that discipline to my business career. Over the years, my team and I have not let mistakes, failures or mishaps get us down. Instead, even when a venture has failed, we try to look for opportunities, to see whether we can capitalize on another gap in the market ...Business opportunities are like buses, there's always another one coming," says Branson.

And the moral is, it pays to pick your battles carefully. Are you sure you can win your must-win battles?

63. WITH FRIENDS LIKE THESE...

Joe Goyder was insight manager at PepsiCo when Walkers launched Red Sky crisps. It was something he was very proud of, something he dropped into conversation. He took packets home and told his family and friends it was something he had helped invent. He could, and did, enjoy West Country Bacon and Cream Cheese flavour, a Red Sky variety he thought was the best crisp flavour ever invented.

That was until 2014 when Walkers dropped the brand.

Looking back, Joe recalled that the brand had had a bright start.

"We had a solid strategic foundation. In the UK, Walkers had been losing share to Kettle, Burt's and the other premium crisp brands for months, and it was clear that we either had to buy them or beat them, so we attempted the latter. We used the data available to us pretty intensively to understand the market – precisely who, what, when and where premium crisps were being eaten, and how to win.

"We overcame some interesting issues with our concept/product fit. Our initial plan, to create a traditionally British crisp brand, didn't work. Traditional Britishness led consumers to expect thick crisps, and our factory only made thin crisps, so instead, we worked with AMV to develop a positioning based on Rural Optimism. From there, it was a short creative hop to "Red Sky at Night – Shepherds' Delight". "Shepherds' delight" clearly wasn't going to work, so after some contemplation and some great quant results, we settled on Red Sky as name. Our concept/product testing proved that the brand had the potential to win, and we were all set for a launch.

"We worked with Ziggurat to create a great pack design, and AMV made a rather charming advert – all thoroughly validated and optimized through quant research."

It was then that, as Joe himself says, "things began to get complicated".

As well as confirming the Red Sky positioning, the research had highlighted that some consumers felt the thin crisps 'weren't rustic at all, (they were) just like crunchier Walkers crisps'.

Hearing this, Walkers decided that they might have two ideas rather than just one, and perhaps there was an opportunity for 'Walkers Extra Crunchy' as well.

Joe picks up the story: "At first we were excited that our brand creation project had sparked not one, but two brand ideas. Unfortunately, we'd also created our biggest competitor.

"Partly as a consequence of this, our launch budget was reduced. This was done for sound commercial reasons, but it's an important consideration for anybody thinking of creating a new brand. A new brand, with low levels of awareness, is unlikely to have the same media efficiencies as a well-known brand. Within the Walkers portfolio, our little brand was never a priority, and never received the budget we'd hoped for, it went instead to Walkers Extra Crunchy. My reflection is that new brands are a bit like babies – creating them is more fun than supporting them. Marketers who think they want them at the start of the process may reconsider their decision when they come face to face with the maintenance bills.

"So in essence, we created a great little brand, which delivered its targets for five years, but in the process we created a Walkers sub-brand which stole our marketing budget and line capacity."

With a friend like Walkers Extra Crunchy, Red Sky didn't need enemies. And rather than shepherd's delight, perhaps they should have known that the Red Sky was a warning.

And the moral is, sometimes your competition will be on your own doorstep. How do you ensure you are your company's best option?

64. IT'S NOT A PROBLEM, IT'S AN OPPORTUNITY

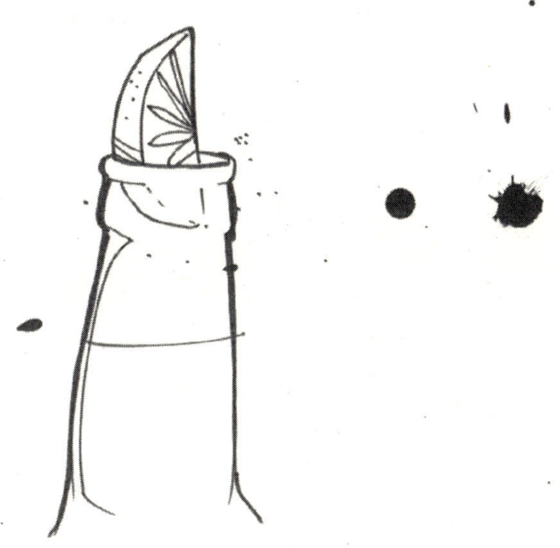

Corona, which means 'crown' in Spanish, is the number-one selling beer in Mexico, number-one imported premium beer in the US, and the number one selling Mexican beer in the world.

It was launched in 1925 in a clear glass bottle and, after a few early problems, the marketing team considered the possibility of changing to a dark glass bottle, to make it easier to preserve the flavour. In the end, they rejected the idea and retained what has become the iconic transparent bottle.

It was a decision that has ultimately proved to be key to the success of the brand, but perhaps not in the way they expected.

Those early problems with preserving the flavour were down to what is known in the brewing industry as the beer being 'light-struck'.

A beer becomes 'light-struck' when it has been exposed to ultraviolet and visible light for an extended period. The light causes the vitamin riboflavin, which is present in beer, to react with and break down isohumulones, which are the molecules that contribute to the bitterness of the beer and are derived from the hops.

The resulting molecule, 3-methylbut-2-ene-1-thiol, is very similar chemically and in odour to the musk-borne mercaptans that are a skunk's natural defences. The net result of which is that light-struck beer is often said to be "skunked" or to taste "skunky".

It is to prevent this problem that most beers on the market are served in dark bottles, and indeed other leading Mexican beers like Dos Equis and Tecate have always been produced in brown bottles.

Corona, however, had decided to persevere with its clear bottle and hope that any problems would be minor.

All went well and the brand flourished, becoming the number one beer brand in Mexico in 1935. However, when the brand started to be shipped to the US in 1976, after the long journey and exposure to the sun, some people started to complain about the taste.

The team at Corona, feeling that their distinctive bottle was by now a well-established equity of the brand and hoping that any problem with light-struck beer wouldn't be too widespread, decided to stick with the clear bottle.

Instead of changing the bottle or trying to address the cause of any problem, they looked for ways to mask it if it happened. They hit upon the idea of putting a wedge of lime in the neck of every bottle to sweeten the flavour and hide any possible 'skunky' taste.

The solution turned out to be better than they could have ever imagined; not only did it overcome the taste problem, it led to a huge growth in sales. Corona had created, almost inadvertently, a drinking ritual which was to give them a real point of difference. Corona soon became the number one imported beer in the US and is now available in over 180 countries around the world.

The bottle with a wedge of lime protruding from its neck is now a well-established communication equity for the brand. So much so, that they tried to register the image of a clear bottle with a slice of lime in the neck as a community trademark, but, on 30 June 2005, the European Court of Justice rejected it as indistinctive.

Not surprisingly, many other Mexican beers have now adopted the wedge of lime ritual, but Corona still remains the leading Mexican beer brand.

And the moral is, good brands can turn a problem into an opportunity. What problem could you use to your advantage?

Footnote: There are a number of other stories that claim to explain why a lime is used. Some say that squeezing a lime into a Corona beer is a time-honoured Mexican custom to improve the beer's taste. Some say that the ritual derives from an ancient Meso-American practice designed to combat germs, with the lime's acidity destroying bacteria. Others say that the lime is used to keep flies away from your bottle. However, while a Corona is always served in the US and in many other countries with a wedge of lime, in Mexico that same bottle of beer would likely be served that way only in a bar frequented by Americans. Mexicans who drink Corona tend to scoff at the idea that the beverage needs a lime, regarding the fruit's addition as a gimmick for "los turistas". Furthermore, if you look at the early advertising developed for the Mexican market prior to the 1980s, there is no lime sticking out of the bottles, suggesting that the story I have told here is perhaps a more likely explanation.

65. FRIENDS IN HIGH PLACES

The Jelly Belly Candy Company owes a lot of its success to friends in high places.

And they don't come much higher than the US president, unless you count the astronauts who made them the first jelly beans in space.

In 1967, Ronald Reagan was serving his first term as California's governor and was in search of something to help him quit smoking. He wanted something low in fat, not too high in calories but with enough flavour to ward off his nicotine cravings. He found the perfect snack in jelly beans.

For nine years, just about any jelly bean would do, but that was to change in 1976 when a San Francisco company started to make a new kind of jelly beans – that were more intensely and naturally flavoured. Reagan converted to the new Jelly Belly beans made by HG Candy Company. He became their most famous fan.

When Reagan was elected president in 1981, he wanted the beans served at his inaugural festivities, but there was a problem. Not surprisingly, the colour scheme for the inaugural was red, white and blue, and while there were red, yellow, white, orange and black Jelly Bellies, there wasn't a blue one.

HG Candy Company immediately started work on developing a new blue variety, and after much testing, a blueberry Jelly Belly was agreed.

In the end a total of 3 ½ tons of red, white and blue Jelly Bellies were shipped to Washington, DC for the festivities, and with roughly 800,000 candies per ton, that was some 2,800,000 Jelly Belly beans.

They were served in the Oval Office, and were a must have for cabinet meetings. They travelled with the president on Air Force One, and a special holder was designed for the plane so the jar would not spill during turbulence.

In 1983, President Reagan sent a surprise gift to the astronauts on the Challenger shuttle – Jelly Belly beans, of course. They became the first beans in space.

When Reagan died in 2004, black ribbons were attached to the large jelly-bean mosaic portraits of Ronald Reagan which hang at the Jelly Belly Candy Co, and mourners left little packets of jelly beans in his presidential library.

HG Candy Company chairman is in no doubt, Reagan's love for the candy "made us a worldwide company overnight".

And the moral is, friends in high places and in the public spotlight are friends indeed, and are worth cultivating. Which famous person could be a brand advocate for you?

Footnote: While blueberry remains one of the most popular flavours, it was not Reagan's favourite. That honour goes to the black liquorice-flavoured bean.

66. FROM BAGS TO RICHES

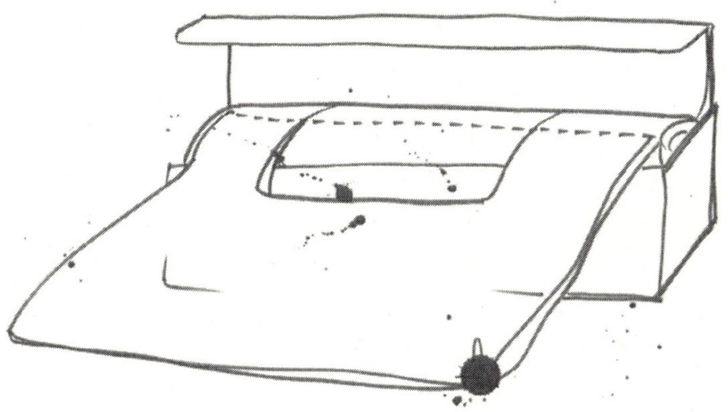

How does a brand that sells kitchen gadgets through that most impersonal of channels – direct mail – and conducts no market research become a beacon for best practice when it comes to customer service?

Alan Rayner was the founder and his initial business was selling agricultural plastics: covers for haystacks, silage sheeting, Lammacs – plastic coats to protect new-born lambs and, most famously, plastic bags for chickens. The business, originally known as Lakeland Poultry Packers, is now known simply as Lakeland.

In 1974, when Alan retired, his three sons, Sam, Martin and Julian Rayner, took over the business. One of the first things they did was to change its direction. It was a decision that laid the real foundation of the brand today.

Home freezing was the 'in thing' in the 1970s, and the brothers had "a moment of inspiration [that] told us people who froze food also cooked it! So along came the 'Everything for Home Cooking' catalogue. We scaled down the agricultural side and headed in the direction of all things kitchenware". It proved to be a great decision.

It's a company constantly bringing new products to the market. It puts out up to 18 catalogues a year, containing 3,500 products related to homeware, cleaning, crafts and Christmas. It has about 70 stores in the UK and a thriving internet business.

Not long after the brothers took over, Michelle Kershaw joined them. She quickly learned everything there was to know about home freezing and kitchenware, and became their resident expert and the face of Lakeland.

She went on to become their customer director but, as Julian readily admits: "Michelle was Lakeland. She had a huge personality, huge confidence. You couldn't replace her. If something wasn't right, you knew about it from Michelle. She would speak up for the customer."

Never much of a cook, Michelle had a passion for cleaning. Every Friday, she would take home a bag full of products and test them over the weekend. If she thought something was "crap", she would say so, but, if it did its job, she wanted to tell her customers.

Michelle would always be in the office at 7am brewing a litre of coffee. "She never looked less than perfect and had a room the same size as her bedroom full of glitzy clothes," says her PA, Barbara Shepherd. "You had to be careful about admiring anything because she would give it to you – she was that generous."

Lakeland customers were her friends. They rang her when their dogs died, they came to visit her in Windermere and sent cards. If they found a wonderful product on holiday, they couldn't wait to get back and tell her – the soft liquorice from Australia that is selling by the ton started as a customer suggestion.

This meant that the company didn't, and doesn't, need to conduct formal market research, as it talks directly to customers.

Michelle was diagnosed with lung cancer in March 2003, yet, despite her illness, she continued working long hours. She was told that she needn't and shouldn't come in before 8.30am, but she came in early as always.

Later that year she was given the Lifetime Achievement Award for services to the home shopping industry.

On the day before she died in 2004, Michelle was driven to the office in the afternoon. Too weak to get out of the car, she checked proofs in the car park. Next morning, her last act was to finish a customer letter.

When told of her death there was a huge, heartfelt out-pouring of grief from customers.

And the moral is, the best brands understand and look after their customers. What do you do to truly look after your customers?

67. HOW A PUNK AND A DWARF CHANGED THE BREWING WORLD

James Watt is a self-proclaimed punk. He doesn't pull his punches; he tends to go in both – beer – barrels blazing.

In his book *Business for Punks*, he describes the launch of his brand: "Rewind to 2007. Based in a shed, on a remote and godforsaken industrial estate in north-east Scotland, BrewDog came howling into the world. Martin Dickie (my best friend) and I set up one tiny brewery with one very big mission: to revolutionize the beer industry in the UK and completely redefine British beer-drinking culture."

Their purpose was, and still is, to make other people as passionate about great craft beer as they are.

Since the launch, the brand has gone from strength to strength. From two humans and a dog, BrewDog now employs more than 500 people. Its beers are exported to over 50 countries, and it now owns and operates over 40 BrewDog craft beer bars in some of the coolest cities around the world. For the last four years, it has been the fastest growing food and drink producer in the UK.

It has done it all in its characteristic unconventional in-your-face-style. "You need to get incumbent companies, competitors, random people and, in our case, regulatory bodies to completely hate you."

The year was 2010, and BrewDog decided it wanted to serve their craft beers in two-third pint measures in their UK bars. They felt this was a better size to showcase some of their stronger and more complex beers. It also fitted with the UK government's desire to promote responsible drinking.

What BrewDog didn't realize was that it was up against a 300-year-old piece of licensing legislation which outlawed the two-thirds measure.

James and his team tried writing to parliament and lobbying politicians, but conventional methods got them nowhere. They decided to adopt a more unconventional alternative.

They hired a 4ft 5in dwarf dressed as a punk and, armed with an array of placards bearing slogans like "size matters" and "small for all", they started a week-long protest at Westminster and 10 Downing Street. They called it "the world's smallest protest". A petition and social media campaign were simultaneously launched.

It worked. In 2011, science minister David Willets confirmed that the coalition government would change the rules and allow the introduction of the new two-thirds of a pint measure, sometimes known as a 'schooner'.

On hearing the news, James Watt said: "The craft beer revolution has claimed another scalp in the form of archaic licensing rules. This is nothing short of a landmark victory for BrewDog and an acceptance at government level that we speak for the people and understand the changing landscape of the UK beer market. The two-thirds of a pint measure means British beer drinkers can enjoy bold and creative beers responsibly – we knew that and we made sure the government caught up."

And finishing off in his understated way on the BrewDog blog, he went on to comment: "If we weren't so busy brewing, we would probably be able to solve most of the world's problems."

And the moral is that new brands may need to start a revolution, not just a business. What revolution do you want your brand to lead?

68. FROM TOOTHPASTE TO GLOBAL ELECTRONICS – LUCKY BY NAME BUT BRAVE AND BOLD IN DEED

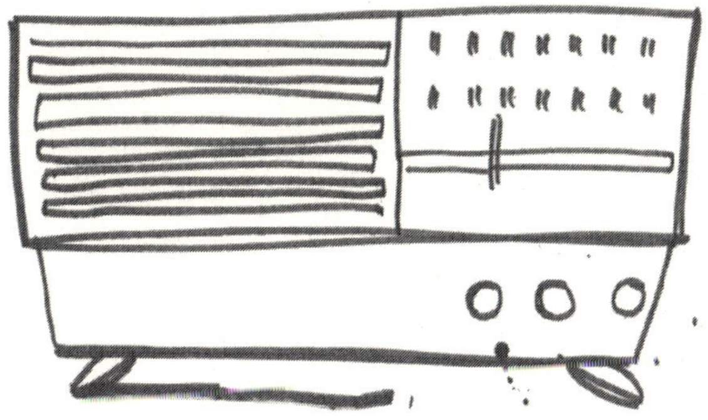

Lak-Hui Chemical Industrial Corporation had been founded in 1947. Pronounced Lucky, it produced hygiene products such as soaps and laundry detergents and was most famous for its Lucky and Perioe toothpaste brands. In 1952, it had become the first Korean company to enter the plastics industry.

In 1957, Yoon Wook-Hyun, planning director of Lak-Hui Chemical Industrial Corporation, was attending a meeting of other managers, executives and the company's founder and president, Koo In-Hwoi.

He made what, he thought, was just an innocent comment: "Nowadays, I find myself spending my evenings listening to the radio."

Much to everyone's surprise, Koo In-Hwoi responded with: "We could make radios."

The late 1950s was a period of dramatic technological change, with radios being seen as an embodiment of modern civilization, bringing news of the world to Korean listeners. However Korea was still struggling to rebuild itself post the Korean War and the notion of a Korean company making radios seemed a long way off.

Politely Yoon Wook-Hyun voiced what most of the executives were thinking: "I wouldn't say it's impossible, but our technology is too far behind."

Koo In-Hwoi wasn't to be dissuaded, he was sure that it was something they could and indeed should be doing.

"We could certainly deal with it. If we need to learn, we'll go abroad and learn; if we can't, we'll invite foreign technical experts here. I say let's unveil the electronic industry within Korea."

Later that year, on 1 October 1952, Luk-Hai founded a new company, GoldStar, and work started in the new design laboratory on what was to become the A501 radio.

While importing radio components would have been more practical than risking in-house development, it was decided that GoldStar would develop its own components domestically. It was a bold decision, one that took a long-term view of the industry's potential rather than looking to solve the immediate short-term challenge. It was a decision that helped lay the foundation for the company to become a major player in technology. GoldStar began to produce its own switches, transformers and sockets, and on 15 November 1959, the first A501 radio came off the assembly line.

Keen to build on this success and not scared of making brave choices, GoldStar started to develop its second radio. It decided to use the emerging new transistor technology, and created the T701. Unfortunately, the new technology meant the price of the new radios was much higher and sales were terrible. GoldStar was teetering on the edge of disaster. But, the company had a stroke of luck, on 16 May the military government announced a plan to supply radios to rural and farming areas and gave a contract to GoldStar. Sales, which had been just a few thousand in 1960, rose to over one million in 1961. In 1962, GoldStar started exporting some of its radios, gaining extra income and valuable foreign currency.

GoldStar, now on a stable footing, went on to produce Korea's first domestic TVs, refrigerators, washing machines and air conditioners.

It was later merged with Lucky to form Lucky-Goldstar, and in 1995, in a move designed to help it compete even more effectively in Western markets, it was renamed "LG".

And the moral is, the best brands dream big and set themselves audacious goals. What could you do if you stretched your thinking?

COMMUNICATION

In the past, communication between brands and their customers was one-way: The brand advertised to its audience trying to sell to them on their brand's benefits often in a style that could only be characterised as adult to child.

Nowadays things are very different: the audience is not only media literate but marketing literate too. People don't want to be sold to, they want to be able to engage in dialogue, in conversations. There are many more media channels: the internet and social media facilitate engagement to an extent that could have hardly been envisaged 30 years ago. Consumers create their own branded content to such an extent that for some brands it is more than they put out themselves

The stories here cover tales from the glory days of *Madmen* advertising, to more recent tweets from customers, from campaigns that ran for years, and from some that nearly didn't run at all.

69. SANTA CLAUS AND THE BACKWARDS BELT

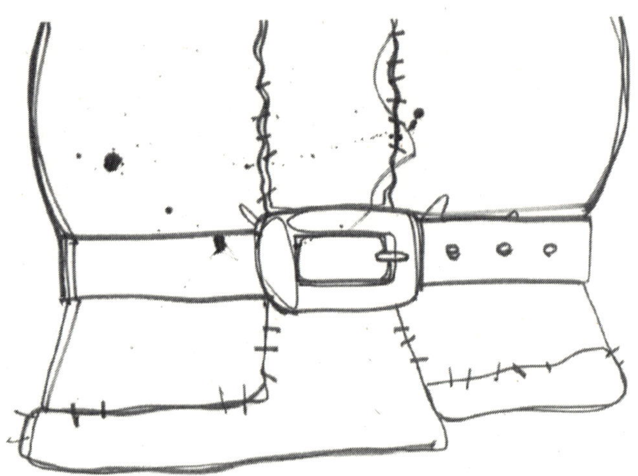

Coke has long been associated with the Christmas period, and in particular with the depiction of Santa as a jolly, white-bearded, old man dressed in a red-and-white outfit. Indeed, many believe that Coke 'invented' this modern day depiction of Father Christmas as a 'branded' re-incarnation of earlier green-coated figures.

The truth is a little bit different. Father Christmas had historically been depicted in many ways, and often as an elf-like figure in a green coat. But he had started appearing dressed in red and white at the turn of the 20th century, most notably on covers of the popular magazine *Puck*.

Coca-Cola was the brand that consistently and widely used the image, and helped to popularize it. But it was not the first soft drink brand to use the 'modern' image of Santa Claus in its advertising. That particular honour goes to White Rock Beverages, who used a red and white Santa to sell its mineral water from 1915 onwards, and from 1923 he was promoting both the company's mineral water and ginger ale.

Coke's association with the red and white Santa really began in 1931 when Archie Lee, a D'Arcy Advertising Agency executive, convinced the company that it needed a campaign to show a wholesome Santa who was both realistic and symbolic.

Michigan-born illustrator Haddon Sundblom was commissioned to develop advertising images showing the real 'Santa', not a man dressed up as him.

Sundblom took his inspiration from Clement Clark Moore's 1822 poem *A Visit From St Nicholas*, which is much better known as *Twas the Night Before Christmas*. It was Moore's description of his St Nick that Sundblom used to create his warm, friendly, pleasantly plump and human image of Santa.

Sundblom asked his friend Lou Prentiss, a retired salesman, if he would pose – and Prentiss was the model for the first few Sundblom ads. Images that proved immensely popular. Unfortunately, Prentiss passed away.

After considering a number of options, Sundblom decided to use himself as his next model – and to facilitate this he used a large mirror. Which would have been OK if people had not loved the images so much, and paid such close attention to them, because after the next ad went out, Coca-Cola received a sack full of letters asking why Santa's belt was backwards. Sandblom had forgotten to transpose his painting.

Sundblom learnt his lesson, and while he continued to use real life models and props, he made sure he made any adaptions required.

Two children who appear with Santa in a number of Sundblom's paintings were based on Sundblom's neighbours – two little girls; but because he knew people would prefer it, he changed one to a boy.

In his 1964 painting, Santa is seen with a dog, which was actually a grey poodle belonging to the neighbourhood florist. However, to make sure the dog really stood out in the wintry (white) scene, Sundblom painted the animal with black fur.

Part of the appeal of his images was that they were realistic, even if they weren't always exactly true to life.

And the moral is that you don't have to be first to market – size, spend and commitment can be more important. Where could you still win even if you aren't first to market?

Footnote: Another related myth that isn't true is that "Sprite Boy", a character who was introduced in 1942 and who appeared with Santa Claus in Coca-Cola advertising, was named after the Sprite brand. However, Sprite Boy, who was also created by Sundblom, got his name due to the fact that he was a sprite, or an elf, and it wasn't until the 1960s that Coca-Cola introduced the actual Sprite brand.

70. A TAGLINE IS FOREVER

In the 1930s, presenting a woman with a diamond engagement ring when proposing was not the social norm, whereas this is almost always expected nowadays. The Great Depression had made matters even worse for De Beers, the brand that controlled 60% of rough diamond output. Sales that had been declining for more than two decades, plummeted even further.

De Beers decided to embark on what it now describes as a "substantial" campaign, linking diamonds with engagement. The firm hired Philadelphia-based advertising agency NW Ayer in 1938 to try and make Americans fall in love with diamond engagement rings.

At the time, only 10% of engagement rings contained diamonds, and they were seen as an extravagance for the wealthy.

The challenge Ayer faced wasn't easy. As internal Ayer documents later observed, the campaign required "the conception of a new form of advertising, which has been widely imitated ever since. There was no direct sale to be made. There was no brand name to be impressed on the public mind. There was simply an idea – the eternal emotional value surrounding the diamond."

The new campaign was to weave together two strands.

The first strand was to suggest a diamond's worth and manage expectations as to what a man should pay for a diamond by suggesting, at least in the 1930s and 1940s, that it should be equivalent to a single month's salary. A figure that would obviously go up with inflation, but which has also been increased to two months in the 1970s and 1980s, and more recently has become three months' salary.

The second strand happened in 1947 when, at a routine morning meeting, Frances Gerety, a young copywriter, suggested a new tagline. Her colleagues weren't particularly impressed. The all-male group felt it didn't mean anything, and that it wasn't even grammatically correct.

Gerety who had been working on the De Beers account since 1942, had often explored ideas of eternity and sentiment. Her previous ads, which had appeared in publications like *Vogue*, *Life*, *Collier's*, *Harper's Bazaar* and the *Saturday Evening Post* had suggested things like: "May your happiness last as long as your diamond." Or: "Wear your diamonds as the night wears its stars, ever and always… for their beauty is as timeless."

Her new line: "A Diamond is Forever" was the summation of her thinking, and was the turning point in the campaign.

Despite those early misgivings, "A Diamond Is Forever" first appeared in a 1948 ad and has appeared in every De Beers engagement advertisement since then.

By 1951, Ayer was seeing success and informed De Beers that "jewellers now tell us that 'a girl is not engaged unless she has a diamond engagement ring'".

In 1956, Ian Fleming's 1956 novel, *Diamonds Are Forever*, the fourth in the James Bond series, was published and subsequently turned into a film with a memorable theme tune of the same name sung by Shirley Bassey.

In 1999, *Advertising Age* proclaimed it the slogan of the century: "Before the De Beers mining syndicate informed us 'A Diamond Is Forever,' associating itself with eternal romance, the diamond solitaire as the standard token of betrothal did not exist," the magazine explained. "Now, thanks to the simple audacity of the advertising proposition, the diamond engagement ring is de rigueur virtually worldwide, and the diamond is by far the precious gemstone of choice."

By the end of the 20th century, 80% of engagement rings contained diamonds because, as all husbands know, she's worth it.

And the moral is, don't underestimate the power of an idea. Is there a big idea that can drive your brand to greater success?

71. THE TIC TAC TOE CHALLENGE

Laura Ellen has a sweet tooth and when she jokingly mentioned her love for a couple of her favourite brands in a tweet: "Can tell I like chocolate a bit too much when I'm following @KITKAT and @Oreo hahahahahah", she didn't know what she was starting.

The folks at Kit-Kat decided, like the gentlemen of honour they are, that the best thing to do was to challenge those "upstarts" at Oreo to a duel for her affection... in a game of Tic Tac Toe (that's noughts and crosses to us, Brits).

So they issued a tweet of their own: "The fight for @ Laura_ellenxx's affections is on. @oreo your move #haveabreak", and a link to a picture of a classic Tic Tac Toe grid in which the middle square was filled with a cross, made up of two delicious looking fingers of Kit Kat.

They didn't have to wait long for a reply (well, about seven hours to be exact). What would be Oreo's move? Where would they put their Oreo shaped 'Nought'?

However, when the gentlemen of Kit Kat looked at the reply, it wasn't quite what they had expected.

The link took them to the picture of the very same Tic Tac Toe grid, but there was no Oreo to be seen. Instead the Kit Kat fingers were almost gone, a tiny bit of one remained and a few crumbs.... "Sorry, @kitkat we couldn't resist ... #GiveOreoABreak". You could almost see the chocolate on their faces.

A lovely compliment to Kit Kat and even an Oreo twist on their famous catch line meant this was an occasion where one customer + social media + two brands + a great sense of humour = everyone smiling.

And the moral is, your brand can benefit when it shows it's more than a business. How can you demonstrate that your brand has a human face?

72. THE NO-SELL SELL

HHCL & Partners was the hot agency of the 1990s. The partners appeared on the front cover of the prestigious *Sunday Times Magazine*. It was the first advertising agency to stop calling itself an advertising agency, and re-christen itself a communications agency.

It was to create a number of impactful, and often controversial, campaigns including the 'hit of real oranges (slap)' campaign for Tango, 'the power of pictures' campaign for Fuji, and 'the extra-ordinary launch' campaign for first direct.

They were voted 'Agency of the Decade' by *Campaign* magazine in 2000, but after a series of mergers and a name change to United London, the agency was closed in early 2007.

However, one of the campaigns it created still lives on today, and in fact has become part of the marketing world's vernacular: "doing a Ronseal" – to do what it says on the tin.

Adam Lury, one of the founding partners and planning director recalls:

"We sent several classic 'clever' HHCL ads out to test with the target audience who were predominantly male DIYers and matter of fact men who took a 'no nonsense' approach to life.

"The planner, Ruth Lees, came back to me after the research a bit shell shocked and said 'This target audience didn't like them. In fact, they were proudly boasting that they didn't just not like these ads, they hated all advertising. They wanted nothing to do with any idea.'"

"So I said to her, 'Well don't advertise to them then'.

"She took that thought back to the project team, and from that built the idea of the non-advertising advertising."

So instead of trying to sell to them, Ruth and the team came up with the idea of just telling them, so "Ronseal – it does exactly what it says on the tin" was born.

And the moral of the story is that sometimes the best sell is no sell at all. Do you know what sort of approach works best with your target audiences?

Source: Conversation with Adam Lury

73. ADVERTISING AS A FORCE FOR GOOD

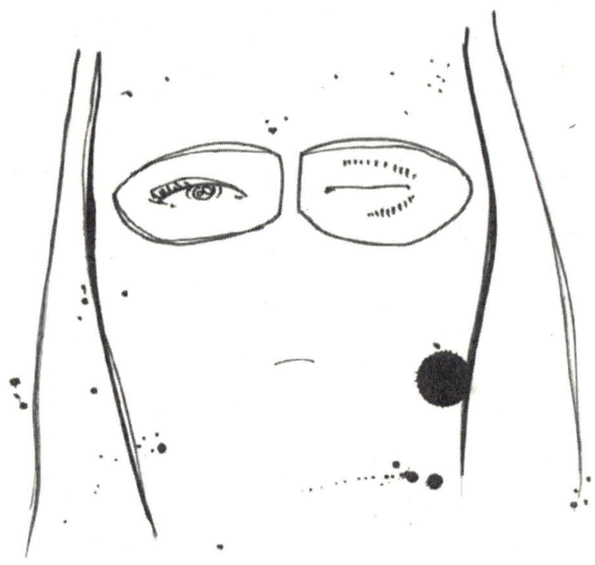

Advertising has a mixed reputation. For some people it is manipulative, even evil; persuading people to buy what they don't need. Many in the industry would however argue that advertising per se is neither inherently good nor bad. It is what it is used for, and how it is used, that defines its inherent worth. Whatever your view, it would be hard to argue that a 2013 campaign run by the King Khalid Foundation and Memac Ogilvy in Saudi Arabia aimed to do anything other than good.

The idea for the campaign started with advertising agency Memac Ogilvy in Riyadh. On its website it explains:

"Women's abuse is a real taboo subject in Saudi Arabia, and is constantly brushed under the carpet. There are no concrete figures as to how many women are abused in the Kingdom as no studies have ever been allowed, but many put the numbers at 92% of married women.

"This rang true closer to home, when a member of the agency confirmed this had happened to someone close to them which concerned us and (we) wanted to help. So how do we create awareness, change and cut through in a country that is very conservative and culturally sensitive, and give women the protection they need, as there is no current law to protect them."

(http://www.memacogilvy.com/casestudy/womens-domestic-abuse-in-ksa/)

The creative team – Jimmy Youssef (copywriter) and Scott Abbot (art director), along with Abdulrahim Bukhmssinand (account manager) and Ossama El-Kaoukji (chief creative officer) – set about creating something that they wanted to be "a proactive campaign that was both controversial, but also paid homage to the culture that exists in Saudi Arabia. A campaign that could only have come from the Kingdom, was a first and [could be] herald[ed] as ground breaking".

The ad they created featured a close-up image of a burqa-clad woman, but when you looked more closely you saw that the women had one 'healthy' eye and one black eye.

Beneath her eyes is a short piece of copy; the English version reads: "Some things can't be covered." The Arabic version, according to Foreign Policy's David Kenner, translates roughly as: "The tip of the iceberg." Underneath were phone numbers for local domestic abuse shelters.

With the idea developed, the team approached the King Khalid Foundation, a not-for-profit organization established in the King's memory by his family. Its aim is to be the leader of the philanthropic and development work in

Saudi Arabia that positively affects peoples' lives, by providing innovative solutions to critical socio-economic challenges in the Kingdom.

The foundation loved the idea and gave its total backing to Memac Ogilvy's "No More Abuse" campaign.

The ad ran in the 17th and 18th April 2013 editions of Saudi national newspapers – *Al watan* and *Al riyadi*, as well as appearing on social media channels, twitter, and Facebook. A website for the campaign included a report on reducing domestic violence and emergency resources for victims.

As expected, and indeed hoped for, the ad instantly sparked a nationwide conversation on domestic abuse and women's rights in the country. It was a watershed moment for women's rights in the country. It was picked up by international news channels and got coverage on both CNN and *Reuters*.

Less than three months after the ad first ran, the Saudi Council of Ministers passed legislation sponsored by the King Khalid Foundation outlawing any form of abuse in the home or workplace.

Today, those convicted of domestic abuse in Saudi Arabia can face a year in prison and a fine of up to 50,000 Saudi riyal (about $13,300).

And the moral is that advertising can be a force for good. How can you use communication to help drive both

74. SOME DECISIONS ARE ONLY FOR THE BRAVE

It's 1964, a time of social turmoil and racial tension in the US.

It's the year of the World Fair that will be held in New York.

It's a key period in the history of SC Johnson, which was at the time a comparatively small Wisconsin-based cleaning products manufacturer.

Herbert Fisk Johnson Jr, the third-generation SC Johnson leader presents his idea to the board.

He suggests they build a Johnson Wax pavilion at the Fair in which they will screen a specially made film. The firm was to use its entire marketing budget on this prestigious one-off event.

And that's not all, he doesn't want the film to be about the company or any of its products, he wants it to be about the simple joy of being alive. His vision is a film designed to celebrate the common ground between different cultures, by tracing how children in various parts of the world mature into adulthood. It was a message of "peace through understanding". The film will be shot in various locations across the United States, Europe, Asia and Africa and feature a multi-racial cast.

Not surprisingly, the other company executives weren't immediately enamoured with the idea. They had numerous questions and challenges.

After politely listening to all their concerns, HF Johnson Jr thought for a while, then simply said: "Some decisions are only for the brave."

The final 20-minute film was shown through an experimental method consisting of three separate 18-ft screens. Unlike the Cinerama process that joined three screens into a single unbroken entity, the three screens were separated by one foot of space.

"To Be Alive!" quickly became one of the fair's most popular exhibits. The public loved it. People lined up around the block to get a chance to see a screening.

Years later, Fisk Johnson, HF's grandson recalled: "My grandfather, HF Johnson Jr, wanted to counter the negativity that was so apparent during this period of American history. He succeeded, bringing a new generation a message of hope and optimism."

"It really put SC Johnson on the map … even though we didn't market our products at all," says Kelly Semrau, SC Johnson's head of sustainability.

And the moral is that it can pay to be brave. What act of bravery could put your brand on the map?

75. IF YOU PAY FOR HALF, I'LL PAY FOR THE OTHER HALF

It may seem almost inconceivable, now but one of the most famous ads of all time – the Apple Macintosh 1984 spot – very nearly didn't run.

The story of its route to the Advertising Hall of Fame begins in late 1982 with Apple's advertising agency, Chiat/Day, working on a print campaign, not for the Macintosh but for its predecessor, the Apple II. The concept was intended to play off George Orwell's totalitarian vision of the future.

Six months before we [even] knew about Mac, we had this new ad that read: "Why 1984 won't be like 1984," creative director, Lee Clow, remembers.

The ad never ran, and that might have been the end of it had it not been for Steve Hayden, a copywriter, and Brent Thomas, an art director, who in the spring of 1983 were looking for some hook to make a bold statement about the new Macintosh. They remembered the ad, and with considerable reworking they put together a storyboard of what would become the 1984 commercial.

This original script described an athletic young woman, chased by helmeted storm troopers, bursting into a dark auditorium in which row upon row of identical workers sat watching an image of 'Big Brother' droning on and on. The heroine would smash the screen with a baseball bat (this was later to be changed to a sledgehammer for dramatic effect) and a refreshing burst of fresh air would pass over the workers as they "saw the light".

Over the closing shot, a voiceover would say: "On January 24th, Apple Computer will introduce Macintosh. And you'll see why 1984 won't be like 1984."

The storyboard was presented to Apple's senior marketing team. John Sculley, CEO at the time, was a bit apprehensive, but Steve Jobs loved it. It was just the sort of radical idea he thought the Mac deserved, so Chiat/Day were given the go-ahead to shoot the commercial and purchase one and a half minutes of airtime during the upcoming Super Bowl.

As soon as the rough cut was ready, Chiat/Day presented it to Jobs and Sculley. Jobs loved the commercial and Sculley thought it was crazy enough that it just might work. In October, the commercial was shown at Apple's annual sales conference and the response was overwhelmingly positive.

In late December, marketing manager Mike Murray was tasked with showing the commercial to the other members of Apple's board of directors: A C "Mike" Markkula Jr, Dr

Henry E Singleton, Arthur Rock, Peter O Crisp, and Philip S Schlein. But when the lights came back on, Murray and Sculley were in for a surprise. The entire board hated the ad – Markkula was staring in dumbfounded amazement, and when he finally spoke it was to ask: "Who wants to move to find a new agency?" Sculley recalls, "The others just looked at each other, dazed expressions on their faces...Most of them felt it was the worst commercial they had ever seen."

The board wanted the ad killed, and told Sculley he ought to sell back the airtime they had bought.

Despite being so close to the date, Chiat/Day managed to find a buyer for the 30-second slot immediately, but that still left Apple with a 60-second slot for which it had paid $800,000. The backup plan, if they couldn't find a buyer, was to run 'manuals', a straightforward product-benefit ad.

Jobs however still believed in the ad and decided to seek the support of Steve Wozniak, even though Wozniak normally didn't like to get involved in political issues. Looking back Wozniak recalled, "One evening I was over at the Macintosh group, which I was about to join, and Steve grabbed me and said 'Hey, come over here and look at this.' He pulled up a 3/4-inch VCR and played the ad. I was astounded. I thought it was the most incredible thing.

"Then he told me that the board decided not to show it. He didn't say why. I was so shocked. Steve said we were going to run it during the Super Bowl. I asked how much it was going to cost, and he told me $800,000. I said, 'Well, I'll pay half of it if you will.' I figured it was a problem with the company justifying the expenditure. I thought an ad that was so great a piece of science fiction should have its chance to be seen."

Wozniak's money wasn't needed in the end; emboldened with this extra support, the marketing team decided to go against the board's recommendation and air the ad. So on 22 January 1984, the controversial commercial aired to an audience of 96 million early in the third quarter of Super Bowl XVIII.

The ad was an immediate sensation and generated an estimated $5 million of extra free publicity. All three television networks, and nearly 50 local stations, aired stories about the spot, most replaying the ad.

Apple fed the media frenzy by announcing that the commercial would never be aired again – which isn't strictly true. However, Chiat/Day had already paid the princely sum of $10 to run "1984" at 1am on 15 December 1983, on a small television station KMVT, thereby ensuring that the commercial would qualify for that year's advertising awards.

In 1995, The Clio Awards added '1984' to its Hall of Fame, and *Advertising Age* named it as number one on its list of 50 greatest commercials.

And the moral is, great advertising is sometimes a leap of faith. Are you willing to follow your instincts?

76. THE MEN IN THE HATHAWAY SHIRTS – PART ONE: DAVID OGILVY

It is 1951. In the little town of Waterville, Maine, a small company that had been producing quality shirts for 116 years, decided things needed to change.

The company, CF Hathaway, approached the still relatively young Ogilvy & Mather advertising agency and asked them to develop a print campaign that would help boost their sales.

It was to be the beginning of a long and fruitful association, and the birth of one of the most famous advertising campaigns in the world.

David Ogilvy, creative director, agreed to take the brief. He spent days doing in-depth research on Hathaway, its shirts and its customers. He came up with 18 concepts before settling on the one he liked best.

It was a campaign built around the image of a distinguished man in a series of interesting, glamorous locations, and always dressed in a Hathaway shirt.

So far, so ordinary.

There was more to the campaign, however, as Kenneth Roman pointed out in his book, *The King of Madison Avenue*. It was the first time "that shirt advertising focused as much on the man wearing the shirt as on the shirt itself".

The man in the Hathaway shirt gave the ads a fictional element. They had "story appeal", as Ogilvy would later say.

There was one more twist to the final cut: the man was wearing an eye patch.

Ogilvy, a flamboyant dresser himself, got the idea to try an eye patch from a photo he had seen of Ambassador Lewis Douglas, who had injured his eye while fishing in England. Ogilvy felt the patch might be both distinctive and help dramatize the concept of an aristocratic man with a colourful life. Readers would wonder how the man had lost his eye, and this would add intrigue to the story of the campaign.

So on the way to the shoot, Ogilvy went in a five-and-dime store and bought a few cheap eye patches. When he arrived at the studio, he was still not certain whether or not they would work. He handed them over to the photographer, saying: "Just shoot a couple of these to humour me. Then I'll go away and you can do the serious job."

However, when the photos arrived and Ogilvy saw those with the model wearing the eye patch, he was immediately sure they had something special.

The first "The Man in the Hathaway Shirt" ad appeared in *The New Yorker* and cost $3,176.

It was an instant success.

As well as appearing in other papers, it was mentioned editorially in *Time*, *Life*, and *Fortune*. A cartoon in *The New Yorker* showed three men looking into the display window of a shirt store. In the next panel, they are pictured coming out of the store, all wearing eye patches.

How much the sales of eye patches went up isn't known, but Hathaway's shirt sales doubled in less than five years.

And as Ogilvy said later about the campaign, and the eye patch: "It made Hathaway instantly famous. Perhaps, more to the point, it made me instantly famous."

And the moral is that creative ideas can be borrowed from anywhere. Where will you find your next idea?

77. THE MEN IN THE HATHAWAY SHIRTS – PART TWO: ELLERTON JETTE

It was 1951. Ellerton Jette, president of a little known shirt maker from Waterville, Maine, decided that things needed to change.

He wanted to grow his little business and turn it into a national brand, but he knew he didn't have much money and needed to make every dollar count.

He had heard about the advertising prowess of creative director, David Ogilvy, at the still relatively young agency Ogilvy and Mather.

Jette felt that if he could only get Ogilvy to take the account, he and his company, CF Hathaway, might be able to get the growth they so desired.

So, after thinking long and hard about how he would pitch the idea to a man used to pitching his own ideas, Jette booked a meeting with David Ogilvy.

"I have an advertising budget of only $30,000," he told Ogilvy. "And I know that's much less than you normally work with. But I believe you can make me into a big client of yours if you take on the job."

Not a bad start, but probably not enough to convince Ogilvy.

Jette went on and made two promises. "If you do take on the job, Mr Ogilvy, I promise you this. No matter how big my company gets, I will never fire you. And I will never change a word of your copy."

Jette realized he probably only had one chance to persuade Ogilvy, so decided to try and give the advertising man what he most wanted. Advertising is a fickle business so the promise of a lifelong client would have been a powerful draw. And a client who gave carte blanche in creative development was unheard of – a dream come true for a creative director.

Jette had done what great marketing men do. He had put himself in his target audience's shoes; in this case he put himself in Ogilvy's very smart, probably handmade, loafers and understood what he might want. He then offered it to him.

Ogilvy was flattered and delighted with the promises. He accepted the job.

Ogilvy's subsequent ads helped transform the fortunes of the company. But they would never have happened had it not been for the marketing genius and insight of Ellerton Jette.

And the moral is that the best propositions are based on a real understanding of the underlying needs and motivations of your target audience. How do you dig deeper with your research and understanding of your target audiences?

78. DUTCH COURAGE

The etymology of "Dutch courage" is most often traced back to the Thirty Years' War (1618-48), but there are a number of versions about its exact source. One states that Dutch gin was used by English soldiers for its warming properties in cold weather and its calming effects before battles; another says that English soldiers noted Jenever's bravery-inducing effects on Dutch soldiers and dubbed it "Dutch courage".

If you were to look for a modern source of Dutch courage you'd look no further than the non-alcoholic *erwtensoep* (pea soup) of Dutch brand Unox. It gives courage and reward for the now traditional "*Nieuwjaarsduik*" – New Year's dive – at Scheveningen, the Netherlands' main beach resort.

The very first recorded Dutch New Year's dive, which officially requires the participation of a minimum 25 dive heroes, took place on 1 January 1960 in Zandvoort. A local swimming club decided it would be a good way to start the year, with a plunge in the bracing and refreshing sea.

Five years later it had become a regular but relatively small annual event with hundreds, rather than thousands, participating.

All was to change some 20 years later when, in 1997, an insightful Unox employee recognized the potential in linking the brand, which had long been seen as warming and nourishing, with the event. He suggested sponsoring the dive, rewarding every participant with a free bowl of warming pea soup to counteract the often very cold water-temperatures.

The first "Unox New Year's dive" took place on 1 January 1998 and, with the exception of one year when temperatures were deemed to be too low, it has become an annual and national – even international – event. It is front-page news, and is regularly shown on television. Nowadays the event even attracts tourists from many countries.

On 1 January 2012, with the sun shining over Scheveningen and the temperature a not unreasonable 70C, as midday finally arrived, over 10,000 divers set off wearing their brightly coloured and clearly Unox-branded hats and gloves. Some added other assorted fancy dress. They raced towards the freezing North Sea, all wanting to be the first in the water.

In fact, 2012 was a record-breaking year across Holland with over 36,000 participants in the 80+ "*Nieuwjaarsduiks*" events, including dives in Amsterdam, De Meern, Rotterdam and Wassenaarseslag. Thousands more watched, millions saw these on TV and read about them in the papers.

The Scheveningen event remains the most popular, and Unox remains the lead sponsor of the event. Nowadays the entry fee is €3, but participants receive a goody bag with the now traditional Unox hat, a commemorative pennant and a special edition pack of Unox pea soup. €1 from every entry fee is donated directly to a local good cause.

It is, therefore, both a body-warming and heart-warming event for those brave enough, or still hung over, to take part in, and has further allowed Unox to cement its place in Dutch culture.

And the moral is, the best brands integrate themselves into the community and seasonal occasions. What opportunities exist for your brand to get closer to its local community?

79. REFRESHING THE ADVERTISING – HIT OR MYTH

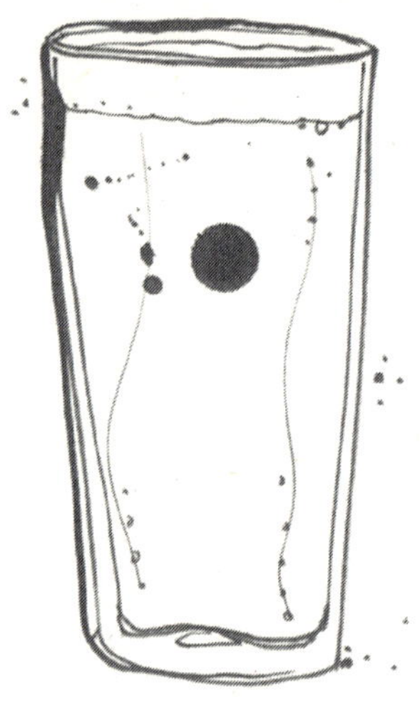

The British love beer. The British love their beer advertising. The British advertising industry loves an advertising myth.

Heineken's famous "refreshes the parts other beers cannot reach" campaign scores on all three counts.

It was the early 1970s, a period when bitter dominated the UK beer market but lager was starting to grow rapidly, and copywriter Terry Lovelock and art director Vernon Howe from the agency CDP were given a brief to create a TV campaign for Dutch lager Heineken. It said just one word – refreshment.

They were struggling to come up with good material. They decided to try new surroundings and headed for Marrakesh. On their way out, they met Frank Lowe, the head of the agency, who told them to make sure they came back with a campaign or not come back at all.

The story continues, according to the book *Inside CDP*: "Lovelock was now desperate. He walked around Morocco with pen and paper in hand searching for the idea. Lovelock said that, 'At the back of my mind, there was a thought that if booze causes some strange metamorphoses, it must be possible to explain its effects on the body in a fun way'. One evening Terry went to bed around midnight, notepad nearby. At 3am, he woke from a dreamless sleep and sat upright. He grabbed the notepad and wrote two lines. 'Heineken refreshes the parts other beers cannot reach' and 'Heineken is now refreshing all parts'. The following morning, he wrote two scripts."

Frank Lowe loved the idea and presented it to the key client, Anthony Simonds-Gooding, then Whitbread marketing director, while the pair were on a flight to St Petersburg.

However, according to the myth, the ads nearly didn't run. The initial market research amongst the public was extremely damning.

But Simonds-Gooding chose to follow his instincts anyway and pressed on. The ads did indeed run and the campaign was to stretch over the next two decades.

Like many myths there is a great deal of truth in this tale, but some parts have perhaps been distorted or exaggerated for effect over the years, so after a little research I can reveal how it really happened.

It is true that Lovelock and Howe of CDP had been given the brief to create a new campaign for Heineken. However, while the key word they were asked to focus on was refreshment – this was part of an overall creative brief, which contained background, target audience and desired tone of voice. However, like many briefs of the time, it was reduced to a single thought or word as shorthand summary of the requirements. The idea that they were only given a single word adds to the drama, but not the truth.

The notion that they just decided to head off to Marrakesh for a change of scene fits with the glamorous and profligate image of the advertising world in the 1970s. However, the real reason they left for Marrakesh was for a photographic shoot for Ford. Without this shoot, their change of scene would probably have been the local pub.

It seems plausible that Lowe might have told them to come back with something or not come back at all – whether he actually meant it was another thing.

Howe, the art director, would have been focused on the shoot, so it's not too surprising that Lovelock, the copywriter, "walked around Morocco" as recalled in the passage from *Inside CDP*.

The next area of controversy is the research and those negative findings. Within marketing circles, the Heineken campaign has long been held up as an example of the tension between creativity and research. It is still quoted as an example of how research can kill a good idea.

Perhaps one of the most interesting points to come to light is that the research everyone refers to took place in April 1974. Yet the campaign first appeared in March 1974 – so the research didn't actually stop it running.

The research itself, contained both negative and positive elements. There were negative comments about the specific executions – 'what's beer got to do with ears?' (Piano Tuner), and 'not the sort of thing you'd like to see when you're eating your tea' (Policemen), and some respondents failed to get the connection between the beer's restorative powers and refreshment – 'beer's supposed to refresh you, they say it's a medicine'.

There was also a respondent's snap judgment about the strapline, which the researcher passed on to the clients and the agency – 'On its own it doesn't stick. No rhythm about it'.

However, more positively, the report also said that the advertising was on strategy, and endorsed the need to focus on refreshment as a point of difference and raison d'être for lager and for this brand.

And the moral is that research provides information and insights that should guide decision-making, not replace it. How have you been using research?

Footnote: When Australian lagers arrived in the UK in the 1980s, Heineken decided it needed to reinforce its European credentials and hired comedian Victor Borge for the voiceovers. This was an interesting choice, since Heineken is Dutch and Borge was Danish, so there is probably another tale to be told.

INNOVATION

The origin of the word 'innovation' is Latin, but could derive from either *innovare* which means to alter/make better, or from *novare* which means to make new.

The stories included in the next section cover both types of innovation, and demonstrate that inspiration can strike at any time or any place. It can be borne out of necessity or from careful analysis.

There are tales of obsessive inventors and meticulous researchers, an unhelpful client and an inspirational chairperson.

All of which goes to prove that there is no one right way to innovate.

80. WHEN ARMAND MET OCTAVE

It is often jokingly said that there aren't many famous Belgians, and the most celebrated are fictional – Poirot and TinTin.

There are, however, two other Belgians who deserve some recognition – Armand Desaegher and Octave Aubecq. Both were successful industrialists in the early 20th century, but their claim to fame arose from their meeting at the Brussels Fair in 1924.

Desaegher was a casting specialist and Aubecq was an enamelling specialist. They decided to work together and combine their skills.

The results were to transform a kitchen staple into a world-wide brand, transforming a commodity into something that was both more functional and more attractive. They added ease of cleaning and visual appeal to the durability of cast iron cookware.

As they developed their first prototypes, they experimented with shapes and colours. The colour they chose, and which is still most associated with the brand, was Flame (an orange colour). Some sources say that the choice was based on a Scandinavian cooker that Octave had seen on his travels.

Whatever the source of that original choice, it was to give their new cookware both the aesthetic appeal that they wanted, but also the inspiration for their name. Once applied and hardened it gave the pots the hue of molten cast iron inside a cauldron or *creuset* in French. The brand now had a trademark colour and name.

Now with a product, a brand name, and what was to become an iconic colour, the partners set up the "Le Creuset" foundry. They chose to base themselves in the French town of Fresnoy-le-Grand, Aisne, Picardy, as it was the crossroads of transportation routes for iron, coke and sand.

The foundry opened in 1925, and the first *Cocottes* (or French ovens) were produced.

Today, Le Creuset is sold in more than 60 countries around the world. The Cocotte is still the most popular item, still produced at Fresnoy-le-Grand and of course still sold in the original orange colour.

Unfortunately for them, Desaegher and Aubecq still don't make most people's list of famous Belgians.

And the moral is that the best innovations have distinctive equities built into them. What equities can you create to integrate within your next innovation?

81. **11 PAGES SHORT**

On 13 January 1888, 33 academics, scientists, explorers and their wealthy patrons gathered at the Cosmos Club, a private club then located on Lafayette Square in Washington DC, to organize a society for the increase and diffusion of geographical knowledge.

After preparing a constitution and a plan of organization, the National Geographic Society was incorporated two weeks later. Gardiner Greene Hubbard became its first president.

The first issue of the *National Geographic Magazine*, as it was originally called, was published nine months later in October 1888.

It was however a rather drab affair, a somewhat dry scientific journal, 98 pages long, wrapped in a brown paper cover that featured a gothic type logo. It contained articles such as, "The classification of Geographical Forms by Genesis", and, "The Survey of the Coast". The only forms of illustration were some meteorological maps, which broke up the black and white text.

For the next 16 years, the format hardly changed, nor did the limited circulation.

However, late in December 1904, the printer told the then editor Gilbert H Grosvenor that 11 pages were unfilled for the January edition and asked what he should do.

In something of a panic, Grosvenor grabbed a package he had recently received from the Imperial Russian Geographical Society. It contained some of the first photographs of Lhasa, Tibet, which at the time was considered one of the world's most exotic places.

He selected 11 of them and sent them off to the printer with instructions to use them to fill the empty pages, despite the fact that in doing so he might face criticism or even be fired.

When the edition came out in January 1905, rather than criticism, Grosvenor was heaped with praise. People stopped him in the street and at the society to congratulate him. The format for the magazine was forever changed, and circulation began to climb. It was to earn Grosvenor the epithet; "the father of photojournalism".

Outstanding photography remains a hallmark of the magazine to this day. Indeed, the front cover portrait of 13-year-old Afghan girl, Sharbat Gula, which first appeared on the June 1985 edition has become one of world's most recognizable photographic images.

And the moral is that sometimes inspiration strikes when you need it most. How can you look at your next problem as an opportunity?

82. **RED THAI AT NIGHT, DIETRICH'S DELIGHT**

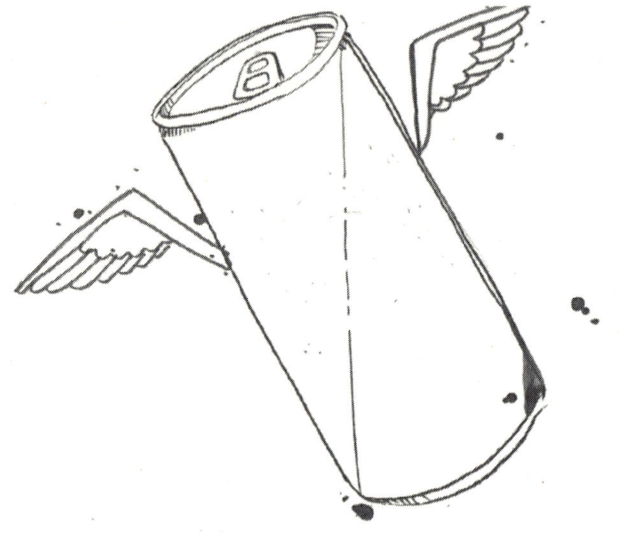

In 1982, Dietrich Mateschitz was the international marketing director for Blendax, a German toothpaste company, and like many international marketing directors he was a perennial globe trotter. While this sounds very glamorous, the reality of constantly travelling the world and criss-crossing time-zones brings with it a number of problems, one of the worst being jet-lag.

On a visit to Thailand in 1982, Dietrich was overjoyed to discover *Krating Daeng*, as here, at last, was something that cured his jet lag. It also turned out to be the source of his future fame and fortune.

Krating Daeng was a sweetened, non-carbonated energy drink which had been developed by Chaleo Yoovidhya and was made with water, cane sugar, caffeine, taurine, inositol and B-vitamins. It was first introduced in Thailand in 1976, and subsequently into other South East Asian countries.

In the early 1980s sales were soaring, especially among truck drivers, construction workers and farmers. Truck drivers used to drink it to stay awake during long late night drives. The working class image was boosted by sponsorship of Thai boxing matches.

Yoovidhya had taken inspiration for the name and the logo from the large wild reddish-brown bovine, the gaur (or in Thai the "*krathing*", "*daeng*" meaning red in Thai). It is a local symbol of power and strength, a perfect association for an energy drink.

Mateschitz, trained in marketing and spotting this opportunity, decided he wanted to work with Chaleo and see if they could take the idea to Europe and the Western world.

Between 1984 and 1987, Mateschitz worked with Chaleos's existing company TC Pharmaceuticals and adapted the formula and composition to Western tastes.

Together they founded Red Bull GmbH in Austria, each investing $500,000 of their savings and taking a stake in the new company. Yoovidhya and Mateschitz each held a 49% share of the new company. They gave the remaining 2% to Yoovidhya's son, but it was agreed that Mateschitz would run the company.

The product was launched in 1987 in Austria, in a carbonated format, and rapidly grew.

In 1992, the product expanded to international markets: Hungary and Slovenia. It entered the United States via California in 1997, and the Middle East in 2000. In 2008, *Forbes* magazine listed both Yoovidhya and Mateschitz as the 250th richest people in the world with an estimated net worth of $4 billion.

And the moral is good ideas travel well. What could you take from elsewhere in the world and bring to your market?

83. WHY RESEARCHERS TRICKED A WOMAN INTO CLEANING HER FLOOR

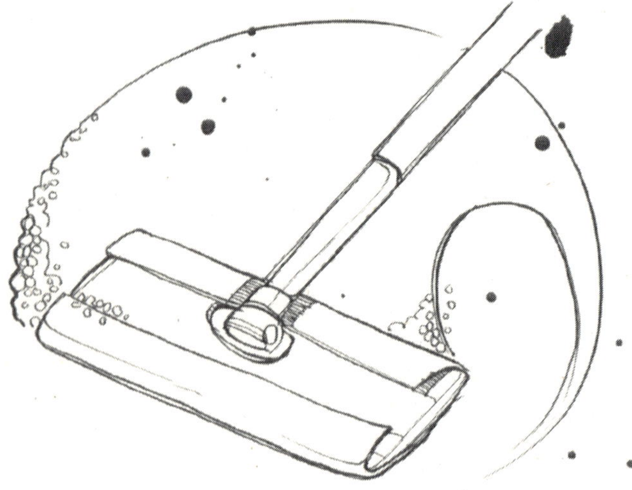

Have you ever really thought about what happens when you mop a floor?

You take your mop and bucket, fill the bucket with water and add your cleaning liquid. Then you plunge the mop into the soapy water and – having wrung it out – start to mop your dirty floor. With luck, you can see the dirt disappearing with every wipe. After a few wipes you plunge your mop back into the bucket and wring it out. Now you're ready to start mopping again, and on it goes till the floor is 'visibly' clean.

Job done...or is it?

Let's think about this whole process a bit more closely. After wiping the floor for the first time you plunge a dirty mop into the soapy water to 'clean it'– the dirt on it comes off, but that dirt doesn't disappear. In fact, it contaminates the clean soapy water making it dirty soapy water.

The next time the mop is plunged into the bucket, even if wrung out, it will come out as a dirty, damp mop and you use it to clean your floor. You're not removing the dirt, you're just moving it around.

It was this thinking that led the director of corporate new ventures at Procter & Gamble (P&G) to say "there has got to be a better way to clean a floor. Current mops are the cleaning equivalent of the horse drawn carriage – where's the car?"

P&G decided it needed to really understand how people cleaned their kitchen floors. Ethnographic researchers were sent into people's homes to watch them clean, dust, wipe and mop.

At first the results just didn't seem quite right; it all seemed too easy. It was then that the researchers realized that many of the people they were coming to watch had already cleaned their house because someone – the researcher – was coming to visit.

The researchers decided they would have to be sneakier. They started arriving with dirty shoes and surreptitiously spilling dirt or dust.

One day, one of the research teams spilled some coffee grounds while visiting an elderly respondent. However rather than breaking out a mop, the grandmother swept up the grounds with a broom and then proceeded to use a damp paper towel to clean up the rest of the fine dust.

In that moment inspiration struck, and the Swiffer was born. An electrostatic cleaning system designed to facilitate both sweeping and mopping with a single mess-free device. It would be a variation on "the razor and blade system" whereby the heads would be regularly replaced.

In the year after its July 1999 introduction, more than 11.1 million Swiffer starter kits were sold.

The Swiffer remains one of P&G's most popular consumer products with annual sales of $500 million.

And the moral is that innovation is born by identifying a problem others hadn't seen before, and sometimes persevering and adapting the research approach until you find it. How can you create a tailored research approach to help identify innovation opportunities?

84. THE PEN FOR READERS, NOT WRITERS

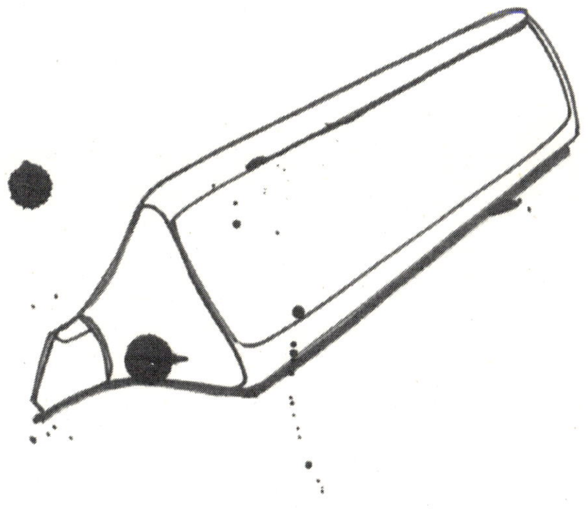

The Stabilo Boss is an unusual pen and an unusual success story. It's a pen designed to help the reader, not the writer. It's the world's best-selling highlighter pen, yet it was wasn't the first highlighter on the market. Its unique design was the result of an act of frustration.

In 1962, Japanese inventor Yukio Horie created a felt-tip pen that used water-based ink. It had a capillary action that pulled the ink through a filter – similar to the one in a cigarette – onto the paper's surface when a writer pressed the highlighter to paper.

The following year, the Massachusetts-based Carter's Ink developed a similar water-based marker, but theirs emitted an eye-catching translucent ink. They called it the Hi-Liter because the see-through yellow and pink inks drew the eye to the text without obscuring what it said. The water- based ink, unlike alcohol-based inks, meant the colour didn't seep through paper.

It wasn't until 1971 that German pen and pencil manufacturer Schwan Stabilo launched its Stabilo Boss highlighter.

Finding the right design, however, proved to be far from easy. With a brief to find something both practical and revolutionary, the in-house designers designed prototype after prototype. All were rejected, until one day, after yet another disappointing presentation, one of the designers in a fit of anger and frustration smashed his latest round-bodied clay prototype into his desk, creating an unusual squat trapezium shape.

Luckily the designer had calmed down enough to recognize that he might now be on to something.

A pen with a round body lets the pen roll and the angle of writing vary according to the writer's grip. The newly flattened body and squared-off nib of the prototype pen encouraged the 'reader' to place it flush to the book or desk's surface. The grip you are forced to use is ergonomically conducive to the sideways swipe that characterizes the act of highlighting.

The shape topped with a bold black lid created the desired revolutionary look setting it apart from other pens and making it instantly recognizable. Originally intended for use in the office to highlight important words, the name 'boss' seems obvious, though nowadays highlighters are used much more widely, in particular in education where students of all ages use it to highlight key passages in texts.

Today 60 million units are produced every year, and two are sold every second.

And the moral is, great design can create innovative new brands. How can you use design to deliver a new or different benefit?

Footnote: One creative-thinking prisoner decided he would try and exchange his prison cell for a hospital bed, at least for a few days, so he 'highlighted' himself in yellow using a Stablio Boss pen hoping that it would give him the appearance of having an attack of jaundice. Unfortunately for him, his guards weren't fooled and all he got was a trip to the showers and not the hospital. "If he had really had such a bad case of jaundice, he would probably have been dead," a prison spokesperson said.

85. THE SPITFIRE, THE UMBRELLA AND THE BABY BUGGY – A STORY OF CROSS POLLINATION

Who would have guessed that perhaps the most famous British fighter plane of World War II would prove to be the inspiration for the world's first and most popular baby buggy?

The connection between the two is Owen Finlay Maclaren and a design he "pulled out of the air".

Born in 1907, Maclaren grew up to become an aeronautical engineer and test pilot. Working for Maclaren

Undercarriage Company Ltd, he invented the undercarriage for the Supermarine Spitfire. His design allowed this famous aircraft to have great manoeuvrability. It allowed the plane to be steered and swivelled easily while on the ground, and for the under-carriage still be folded away neatly and simply when the plane was in the air.

He married and became father to two children, Janet and Colin. Janet married an American airline director and moved to the US, and Colin lived in the UK.

As he neared retirement age, Owen began what he thought would become a slow wind down to a more leisurely lifestyle. All that changed when Janet visited the UK bringing her daughter to see him.

He was delighted and, like many grandparents, spent time taking his granddaughter out and about, to show her off. It was then that he got to experience just how difficult and frustrating it was to manoeuvre a bulky pram.

It got him thinking about how he could rethink, reimagine and reinvent baby transportation. He decided to use his knowledge of aeronautical engineering and applied aviation principles to creating a new 'buggy'.

He decided to use aluminium rods, which had been used in airplanes but, until then, had not been used for household equipment.

He based the framework's structure on triangles for their strength, resilience and flexibility, a trick used widely in airplane production.

He chose double-wheels, which was a feature of landing gear for their manoeuvrability.

Incorporating his own experience of looking after young children and borrowing from another everyday piece of equipment, he used an innovative one-step umbrella-fold type construction. This easy-to-use functionality meant mothers could quickly fold the buggy with one hand, while holding baby in the other. It was to prove a godsend for parents, and was finished with a durable blue and white striped fabric.

Seeing its potential, he applied for a patent on 20 July 1965, for his 6lb prototype receiving Patent No. 1,154,362. On 18 July 1966, he filed for an American patent, receiving Patent No. 3,390,893. The Maclaren brand was born.

The first buggy – the Maclaren B-01 – went on sale in 1967. It was an immediate success and has become a design icon. It has served as the blueprint for every buggy that has been produced since.

Talking about his work a number of years later, he would perhaps subconsciously reference his debt to his aeronautical engineering background, saying: "I very much enjoy my mechanical toys, to be quite honest. It's great fun making new things, dragging some new shape out of the air and then making it work, and then making it. It's the greatest possible fun in my way of thinking."

And the moral is that cross pollination of ideas is a great source of innovation. Keep your eyes open to ideas from afar.

86. **A RUBBISH IDEA?**

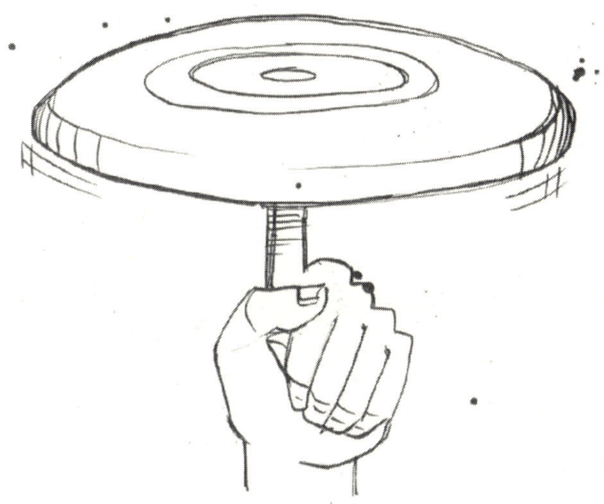

William Russell Frisbie was a baker, and by all accounts a very good one. He was also accidentally the inspiration for one of America's most loved toys.

William moved to Bridgeport, Connecticut, in 1871 to start a new job managing a bakery, a branch of the Olds Baking Company of New Haven. The bakery was a great success and William went on to buy it outright. He established the Frisbie Pie Company and was soon selling his pies all over New England.

William died in 1903, but his son, Joseph, took over and manned the ovens until his death in 1940. Under his direction, the small company grew and shops were opened in Hartford, Connecticut; Poughkeepsie, New York; and Providence, Rhode Island.

Each pie came in a lightweight tin and, while no-one knows who actually threw the first dish, throwing empty Frisbie tins soon caught on, especially amongst the students at Yale and other local colleges. It was here that the distinctive spinning throws were developed. The loud cry of "frisbie!", the equivalent of golf's "fore!" was heard first in New England, and later all across America.

In 1948, Fred Morrison, a Californian buildings' inspector and part-time inventor, had an idea: why bother with the pie, why not just manufacture and sell discs shaped like the empty pie tins? He experimented with welding a steel ring inside the rim to improve the tin's stability, but without success. He then tried moulding a similar shape out of plastic with much more success. He called his invention The Flyin' Saucer, tapping into the craze for UFOs and space travel in general.

Rich Knerr and AK "Spud" Melin, newly graduated from the University of Southern California, were making slingshots in their fledgling toy company when they first saw Morrison's Flyin' Saucers whizzing around southern California beaches. So, in late 1955, they cornered Morrison while he was selling his frisbees on Broadway in downtown Los Angeles, and invited him to their San Gabriel factory where they asked him to join them at the wonderfully named Wham-O toy company. Production started in 1957, and the improved flying saucers were renamed – Pluto Platters.

Sometime later, on a trip to the campuses of the Ivy League, Knerr first heard the term "frisbie". Enquiring about it, he discovered that the students had been tossing pie tins about for years, and called it frisbie-ing. Knerr liked the terms frisbie and frisbie-ing – though Morrison at first was resistant: "I thought the name was a horror. Terrible!"

But Kerr prevailed. Having no idea of the historical origins, Knerr made the decision to go for this name and spelled it "frisbee", phonetically correct, but one vowel away from the Frisbie Pie Company.

By 1982, Morrison had changed his mind and, as he told *Forbes* magazine, now that he had received about $2 million in royalty payments: "I wouldn't change the name of it for the world."

It is estimated that sales of frisbees are now greater than the combined sales of baseballs, basketballs and footballs; not bad for what was originally just a piece of rubbish.

And the moral is, one person's cast-off can be another's inspiration. Have you ever looked at what you do from a completely different perspective?

87. BLUE SKY DRINKING

Given how many military families there are, with generation after generation joining up often to the same regiment, it was perhaps something of surprise when Karan Bilimoria decided he didn't want to follow in his father's footsteps.

Karan's father, Faridoon, had commanded a regiment of Gurkhas when India fought on behalf of Bangladesh in the 1971 war of independence. He went on to become the commander-in-chief of the central Indian army, with 350,000 men under his command.

However, Karan decided the military wasn't for him, and chose to go into business instead.

"If I had followed in my father's footsteps I was worried that I would always be compared to him, and be in his shadow," he said in an interview with the BBC. "I decided that the army for me would have been too constraining … I wanted more blue sky."

And it was with some 'blue sky' (original, creative) thinking that Karan was to make his name.

It was while he was at Cambridge University in the late 1980s that inspiration struck. Karan, like many students, was a lover of beer. But for him there was a problem, none of the existing beers went down well with a curry.

He recalls: "The lager was too fizzy, too harsh and too bloating. It meant that I couldn't eat or drink as much as I would like. At the same time, I found real ale to be great in a pub, but too bitter and heavy with food. So I came up with the idea of creating a beer with the refreshment of a lager, but with the smoothness of an ale."

His idea for what was to become Cobra beer was he "wanted it to not just be drinkable in its right, but a great accompaniment to all food, and particularly Indian cuisine".

Despite having no experience of the beer industry, Karan decided to take his idea to the head brewer at what was then India's largest independent brewery. Luckily the brewer liked the idea, so together they developed the recipe for the smooth-drinking, refreshing lager which would be targeted firstly at Indian restaurants.

The first deliveries from India arrived in the UK in 1990, and came bottled in big 600ml bottles. Without realizing the benefits this would bring, Karan and the head brewer had simply chosen a bottle size similar to other beers sold in India.

Looking back, Karan can now see how this point of difference gave the business an immediate advantage, as the bottles stood out in curry houses.

"People sitting at other tables would see the bottle and say, 'What is that?' The popularity spread like wildfire, people loved the taste, and we got 99% reorders."

The business grew rapidly so, in 1997, brewing was switched to the UK from India to help meet demand. A switch that didn't faze his drinkers: "They didn't mind where we brewed. This is logical as the Indian food you eat here is not flown over from Delhi."

Karan Bilimoria was knighted in 2004 for his services to business and entrepreneurship, and was appointed to the House of Lords two years later.

And the moral is that there is often opportunity sitting in the gaps between existing sectors. Are there gaps between sectors you compete in?

88. SPREADING A LITTLE LUXURY – A FAMILY OBSESSION

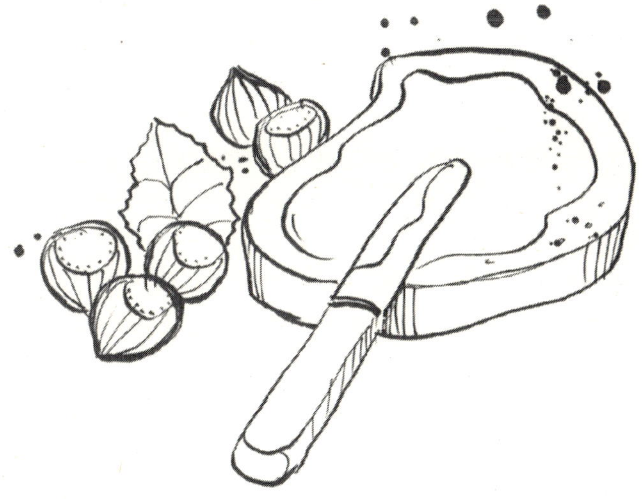

Everyone in Piedmont, Italy, had hazelnuts – lots of hazelnuts.

The region has long been famed for its nut production. However, typically humans don't always value what they have, and in this case what many of the local population really craved wasn't hazelnuts, it was chocolate.

Chocolate was very scarce after World War II. It had been severely rationed during the war, and afterwards was too expensive for most ordinary Italians to afford.

Local baker Pietro Ferrero decided there had to be a solution. It was to become his obsession. He wanted to create an affordable chocolate-y luxury that everyone could enjoy.

He started work on adapting a recipe for "Gianduja" a sweet chocolate confection invented in Turin, during Napoleon's Regency by chocolatier Michele Prochet.

Prochet had been faced with a similar lack of chocolate supply, only his problem was caused by the British Navy's blockade and not World War II. His solution was to extend the little chocolate he had by mixing it with hazelnuts from the Langhe hills south of Turin.

Pietro's idea was to do something similar, but he wanted to find the perfect recipe.

"My grandfather lived to find this formula. He was completely obsessed by it," says the current boss of the family business, Giovanni Ferrero. "He woke up my grandmother at midnight – she was sleeping – and he made her taste it with spoons, asking, 'How was it?' and 'What do you think?'"

In 1946, finally happy with his recipe, Pieto launched Giandujot, or Pasta Gianduja; "pasta" means paste, and "gianduja" is the name of a carnival character famous to the region, a character that Pieto would use in the first advertisements for the product.

Pieto's Pasta Gianduja was made in 'loaves' and wrapped in tinfoil. As it was a soft but solidified block of chocolate and hazelnuts, it had be cut with a knife and the resulting slices would then be placed on bread.

Pieto wasn't completely happy and carried on working away on the recipe, and in 1951 he launched "Supercrema", a spreadable version. Spread-ability was a big step forward. It meant that a small amount went a long way, further helping to break down the perception that chocolate was only for special occasions and celebrations.

Pietro's son, Michele, inherited his father's drive to democratize an affordable everyday chocolate treat.

Giovanni says his father was a man obsessed, just like his grandfather.

"My father said, 'We can push it further, there are new technologies, there are new ways to integrate this winning recipe.' Nutella was born the same year as I was born, 1964, so I have a small brother in the family! And it was not just an Italian success but a European success."

The exact date is a matter of some debate, Giovanni explained as the brand approached its 50th anniversary in 2014. "Legend tells us that the first jar was manufactured out of the factory 50 years ago on 20 April, and the first act of consumption was the 18 May – but there's no scientific evidence!"

The new formulation, whenever it was actually launched, and the new name, gave the product instant international appeal. The name said nuts. It also said Italy (-ella is a suffix common in the Italian language and cuisine – think, mozzarella cheese).

Fifty years on, Nutella is still a major global brand, produced in 11 factories worldwide, and accounting for one-fifth of the Ferrero Group's turnover.

The company is the number-one user of hazelnuts in the world, buying up 25% of the entire world's production. Clearly they see the value of those nuts.

And the moral is, brands can add value to commodities. Do you have access to a plentiful commodity to which you could add value?

89. HOW PEUGEOT FOUND SUCCESS WITH A DETOUR VIA THE KITCHEN TABLE

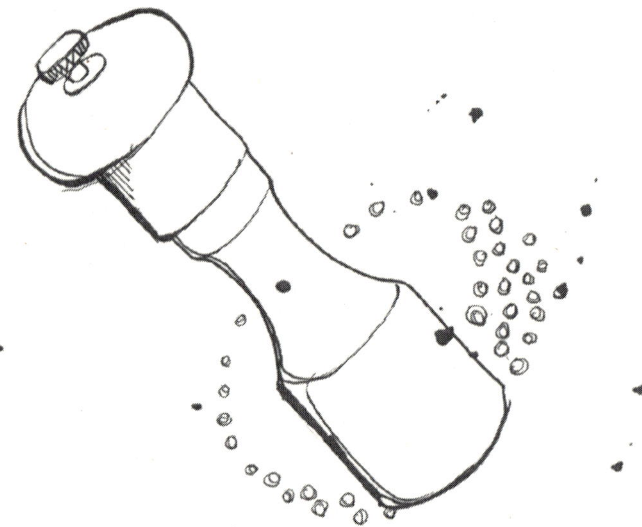

The story of how Peugeot travelled from corset supports in dresses, to motor cars is one of the better-known tales about the brand. However, its detour via the kitchen table that led it to the development of a design classic and the acquisition of its famous lion logo is another enjoyable yarn.

Both stories start in Sochaux, France, where the family lived, and where Jean-Pierre Peugeot had a business manufacturing water mills.

In 1810, The "Peugeot Frères" company was established. Jean-Pierre II, Jean Frédéric Peugeot, Jacques Maillard-Salins and Jean Pequignot purchased a cereal mill at Sous Cratet in the Montbeliard region and set about converting it into a steel factory.

Once completed, the new steel mill started to produce sheet steel and various hand tools, but the firm soon diversified into other areas. These included saws, razors, sewing machines, spectacle frames, clocks, garden furniture and even wire supports for crinoline dresses.

Among the ever-increasing range of steel products produced, the inventive "Peugeot Frères" were most famous for their high-quality saw blades. They had developed a technique of individually cutting the teeth before casehardening the blade. Their process added a carbon-rich alloy to the steel surface for extra strength, and meant the teeth stayed sharper for much longer.

Another diversification was into metal wheel spokes, and wheels. These would lead to the establishment of the Peugeot bicycle brand. Their first bicycle was hand built in 1882 by Armand Peugeot. It was a penny-farthing called "Le Grand Bi".

Soon after, Armand became interested in the new world of the automobile and, following a meeting with Gottlieb Daimler, he became convinced of their potential as a business. The first Peugeot automobile, a three-wheeled, steam-powered car designed by Léon Serpollet, was produced in 1889.

However, before then in 1842, Jean Frédéric would use the blades and simple grinding system – which they had used for a successful range of coffee bean grinders – as the basis to create the classic pepper mill. The design, which has remained pretty consistent ever since, was straightforward and milled the peppercorns to produce a refined powder.

The innovation was perfectly timed, as black pepper, which had been previously known as "black gold", was becoming more readily available and cheaper; the result of the increased frequency of fast ships from south India, and the new railway systems in both India and France.

In the 1850s, the family chose the symbol of the lion as its trademark to reflect the strength of its company's products and symbolize the durability, suppleness and quickness of its metal and steel. The lion also stood for the speed and aggressiveness of the Peugeot company. A lion trademark designed by Justin Blazer, a Montbeliard gold engraver, was registered in 1858.

It was the perfect symbol for Peugeot's pepper mills – intimating that their grinding system was every bit as strong as the mighty animal's jaws. And, of course, it would prove to be a suitable icon for its future cars too.

And the moral is that a technical specialism can be the basis for a wide range of innovations. Do you have a technical expertise that could be leveraged into another market?

90. HAVE YOU HEARD THE ONE ABOUT THE PEDDLER, THE JEWELLER AND THE ATTORNEY?

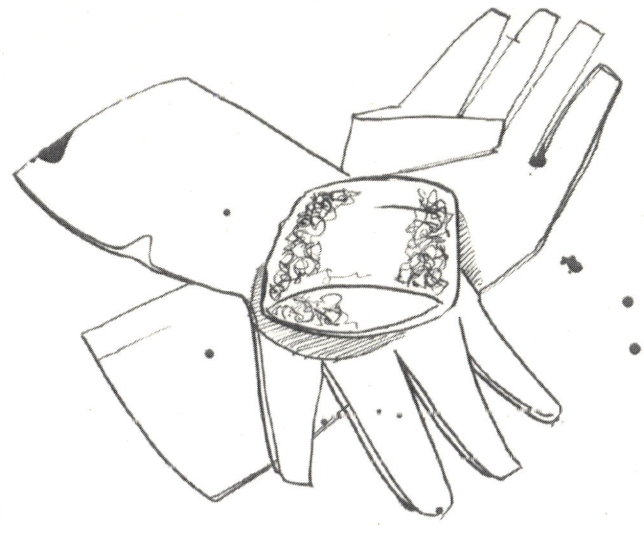

Don't worry it is a clean story. In fact, it's a story about one of the world's most famous cleaning brands. A brand that was turned into an icon by Andy Warhol.

The story starts in the early 1900s, when aluminium pots and pans were starting to replace the traditional heavy cast iron cookware in homes throughout America...but, there was a problem that was slowing the transition down.

The coal-fired stoves of the day quickly blackened the aluminium pots, making them both unattractive and difficult to clean. The new gas stoves of the time weren't much better – depositing soot onto the pans.

A New York door-to-door peddler named Brady found that this problem was limiting his pan sales. He decided he needed to do something about it, so started to experiment with different soaps and rolls of steel wool. He wasn't satisfied with the results he got. The pans were clean but didn't regain their shine.

Brady decided to consult his brother-in-law, a Mr Ludwig, who was a costume jeweller and had different ways and products that he used to clean different metals, glass and jewels of his particular trade. Drawing on this knowledge, Ludwig suggested what seemed obvious to him. Why not combine soap with jeweller's rouge. Now, jeweller's rouge is finely ground ferric oxide and is regularly used as a polish for metals and optical glass, as it helps bring out the maximum lustre and can help create a mirror-like finish.

The resulting combination of steel wool, a bar of soap and jeweller's rouge worked – cleaning and restoring the desired shine.

Brady added the new product to his line of goods. Almost immediately, he found that it was out-selling his pans.

Brady and Ludwig wanted to move into commercial production, and realized they needed to patent their idea. They sought advice from an attorney named Milton Loeb. However, their funds were limited so they offered Loeb an interest in their fledgling business instead of his fee. Loeb obviously saw the potential and not only accepted the stake, he joined the company, going on to become treasurer and president.

It was Loeb who suggested the "Brillo" name, under which the soap bar was duly patented and registered as a trademark in 1913. The partnership formed between the peddler, the jeweller and the attorney became known as the Brillo Manufacturing Company, with its headquarters and production operations in Brooklyn.

By 1917, the Brillo Manufacturing Company was making steel wool pads and packaging them, five pads to a box, with a cake of soap included. In 1921, the Brillo Manufacturing Company moved to bigger premises in London, Ohio.

In the early 1930s, the next – and perhaps most dramatic – step in the brand's evolution happened. The company developed a method of putting the soap into the heart of the pads, creating something close to the classic Brillo pad we know today.

The new soap-filled pads were a success, and Brillo went on to become one of America's most recognizable brands. But it was in the 1960s, when Andy Warhol produced his oversized replicas of the bright, simple and bold packaging, that Brillo became a true marketing icon.

And the moral is that innovation is often the result of mixing different skills and competencies to create something new. What competencies could you mix up to create something new?

91. DIABETES AND A PATIO – THE STORY BEHIND THE STORY

When Diet Pepsi celebrated its 50th anniversary, much of the coverage focused on how it had started life as Patio Soda and featured in the hit TV series *Mad Men*.

While the TV series took some liberties, it was based on the facts.

Royal Crown, a cola maker, introduced Diet Rite Cola in 1958. It was targeted towards the growing number of calorie-conscious women, and proved to be very successful. Successful enough that both PepsiCo and Coca-Cola were forced to act. But not so successful that either one of the companies were willing, at least initially, to link the new diet products to their main brands.

Coca-Cola introduced Tab in 1963, and it was marketed to consumers who wanted to keep 'tabs' on their weight.

Patio Diet Cola was the brand launched by PepsiCo, also in 1963. Fitness promoter Debbie Drake was its spokesperson, and the drink was also marketed as a brand for the calorie conscious.

Early in 1964, PepsiCo released orange, grape, and root beer flavours, but then, later that year, in light of good sales results, Patio Diet Cola became Diet Pepsi. The newly rebranded diet cola was advertised alongside the original Pepsi, with the tagline "Pepsi either way".

Most of the remaining Patio flavours were phased out by the early 1970s, while a few survived until the mid-1970s.

There is, however, another story behind this one. Tab and Patio weren't followers – "me-toos" to Royal Crown's Diet Rite Cola, they were the third and fourth on the market (me-three and me-four).

The original diet soda wasn't even created for the calorie-conscious. It was born as a soft drink for people with diabetes.

The story behind the story goes back to 1904, when Hyman Kirsch, a Russian immigrant, began selling soft drinks in the Williamsburg section of Brooklyn, New York. Some years later, the successful Kirsch became vice president of the Jewish Sanitarium for Chronic Disease (now the Kingsbrook Jewish Medical Center), and he and his son Morris came up with the idea of creating a special beverage for the hospital's diabetic and cardiovascular patients.

Using an artificial sweetener called calcium cyclamate, they created a diet soda and a ginger ale, which they called "No-Cal". No-Cal Root Beer, Black Cherry, Lime and Cola soon followed. They even introduced a chocolate flavour, which was often mixed with a splash of milk by loyal users.

No-Cal was immediately successful, selling over two million cases of soda in New York and Washington DC alone. And by the end of 1953, the beverages were bringing in over $5 million a year. Its popularity went way beyond the customer base its makers had intended. Soon more than half the people buying No-Cal weren't diabetic – they were just watching their weight.

However, Kirsh didn't have the massive marketing clout and national distribution of its larger rivals, and faced with mounting competition from, at first, Royal Crown's Diet Rite Cola, then Coca-Cola and PepsiCo, it disappeared from the marketplace.

No-Cal proved an unfortunate exception to the old marketing adage about the advantages of being first to market.

And the moral is that you don't have to be first to market to succeed. Can you be a late entrant into an existing market and still win?

92. THE UNHELPFUL CLIENT

It's a classic marketing agency or consultancy complaint – a client who doesn't really know what they want but isn't short of opinions about any ideas or prototypes developed. A client who keeps saying (un)helpfully: "Just give me something unique."

Jim Walker had just such a client when he was working on a project known simply as 'Biscuit for Shipton Mill'.

Walker was the joint managing director of Walkers Shortbread and had been approached by Shipton Mill, based near Highgrove in Gloucestershire. Shipton Mill wanted him to develop something using organic flour and locally grown oats.

"We weren't very sure what they wanted. They weren't very sure what they were looking for. We started with a digestive type of biscuit, and an oatcake type of biscuit. We tried an oat-flake sort of oatmeal cookie. We went round in circles, making every combination ... They wanted something unique," he recalls.

"They" included none other than HRH Prince Charles, a high-profile advocate of organic foods, and of course owner of Highgrove. Not a client it is easy to say "no" to.

In the end it took nearly 18 months and 100 different recipes before Jim Walker and his team found something everyone at Shipton Mill was happy with. He may not have been the easiest or most helpful of clients but, like many brand owners, Prince Charles knew what he wanted when he finally saw it (and ate it).

It was of course, The original Duchy Originals' Oaten Biscuit development began on production, but even then Jim wasn't sure how well the product would sell.

"At the time, organics was still really quite way-out and unusual, and maybe a little bit cranky. I thought it was going to be very, very niche. I wondered how well it would sell. I remember [Prince Charles] saying that when he started organics it was very novel, and many of his friends wondered if he knew what he was doing."

Twenty-one years later, the Prince of Wales hosted a reception at Clarence House to mark the 'coming of age' of his little oaten biscuit, now with sales of over 700 million across more than 30 countries.

His vision had come true: "I wanted to show that it was possible to produce food of the highest quality by working in harmony with nature in a way that would benefit environmental and human health, and that I wanted to do so by following agro-ecological principles, adding value to them through the skills of expert and artisan producers, and then to reinvest all of the profits in good causes. And who would have thought that 21 years later our oaten biscuit would have turned into a brand worth £72 million ... and ... would have donated over £11 million to charitable causes?"

In the end it was an idea that literally took the biscuit.

And the moral is that even with a good idea you may need to try and try again before you succeed. What idea do you have that dserves a second chance?

93. MUSIC ON THE MOVE - THANKS TO THE OPERA-LOVING CHAIRMAN

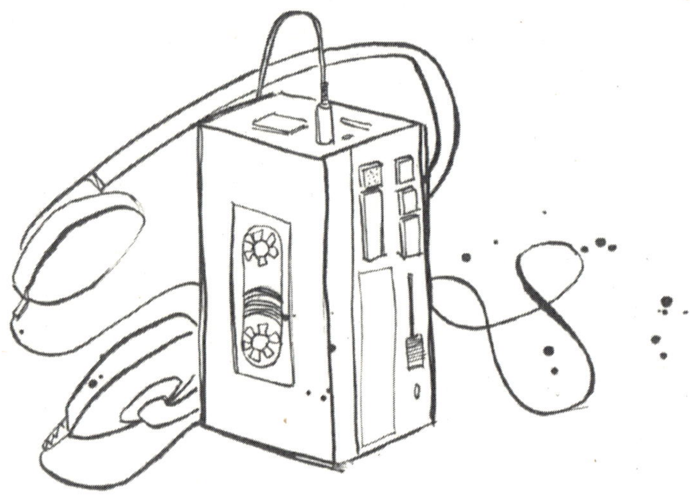

Sony Walkman was created to answer a personal request of the honorary chairman – and went on to be a worldwide success that has helped shape the music industry, selling millions and millions of units worldwide. Later, like Hoover or Sellotape, the name Walkman came to define the category and is listed in the *Oxford English Dictionary*.

Sony introduced the Walkman in 1979, but its origins can be traced back well before then.

The first portable cassette recorders came on to the market in the 1950s, but, like many hi-tech products, they were targeted at a professional market and not the general public. The main users were journalists who could afford the high prices for the equipment and the specialized micro-cassettes, which at the time weren't used in the music industry. Sony called theirs Pressman.

In 1962, Philips invented what became known as the cassette tape, though it was more formally labelled and trademarked as a Compact Cassette. Philips' subsequent decision, interestingly in the face of pressure from Sony, to license the format free-of-charge, led it to become the dominant tape in the market.

1964 saw both the introduction of the first pre-recorded music cassettes and Philips Norelco Carry-Corder 150 portable recorder/player. By 1968, 85 manufacturers had sold over 2.4 million players.

The quality improved dramatically by the early 1970s, and the Compact Cassette went on to become increasingly popular, especially as it provided the ability to re-record.

In 1978, Sony launched the TC-D5 a portable cassette player. While general sales were limited due its high price, lack of lightweight headphones and relatively large size, it did become a favourite among many senior people in the Sony company thanks to its high quality sound.

One regular user was Masaru Ibuka, co-founder and then Sony's honorary chairman. He used the player to listen to operas on his many airplane trips, but he still found the player too heavy for everyday use. He instructed the tape recorder division to create a smaller version.

The division, led by Kozo Ohsone, modified a Pressman to do the job. They removed the record function and added stereophonic sound. Ibuka was immediately impressed and suggested that they bring a similar item to market.

It was a well-timed suggestion: Sony's tape recorder division was flagging. In February 1979, Akio Morita, the company's other co-founder, asked the engineers to develop a similar player that was more commercially viable by 21 June 1979.

With that demand ringing in their ears, and worried that the division would be consolidated into another one if they failed, the engineers went to work. They took a pragmatic approach and designed a portable tape player based on Ibuka's modified Pressman player, but used lower end components to bring the price down and encased it in a small, stylish enclosure.

There was still the problem of the headphones. The current ones were far larger than the new player itself, they weighed more than 400g.

Luckily for the team, three years before, engineers in another division had designed a lightweight pair of headphones. They eliminated the large, enclosed earpiece and in its place put soft foam. They weighed in at around 50g. They were quickly added to the new design.

The device now needed a name. "Walkman", a variation on the Pressman was suggested. It is said that Morita hated the name "Walkman" and feared it would not catch on in the US and Europe. Alternatives, like "Walky", "Freestyle" and "Soundabout" were considered, and even tried in other countries, but ultimately the name Walkman stayed.

Having met the deadline, Sony announced its new product to the trade press on 1 July 1979. The reaction wasn't encouraging. Some claimed that nobody would be interested in a tape player without a record function. Others pointed out that the most popular tape recorder of the time had sold less than 15,000 units, yet Sony had produced 30,000 units.

Sony, however, decided to press on, and the Walkman was announced to the public.

It was the right decision. A month after the Walkman became available in Japanese stores, it was sold out. It went on to be a success right around the world. In the next decade, Sony sold 50 million units, and competitors who copied the idea sold millions more.

The Walkman is now seen as a key milestone along the way to the MP3 players so prevalent today.

And the moral is that occasionally what the chairman wants personally might just be what the market wants. Do you have a personal passion that could be a winner?

REPOSITIONING AND REVITALIZATION

Brands need to stay current and fresh so they don't become tired and out-of-date. Unfortunately, many do wane as times, competition and customer expectations change, so brands have to change too. They have to find ways to rejuvenate themselves.

There are many ways of achieving this: from targeting new audiences, new product development (NPD), developing a new proposition, or finding a new partner. Some undergo amazing conversions, and some have to completely re-invent themselves.

From sickness to health, from female-targeted to an expression of masculinity, from jungle safari to the urban jungle – some of the transformations have stood the brands on their heads.

Rebooted, relaunched and ready to provide learning for others.

94. THE BRAND THAT GOT BETTER

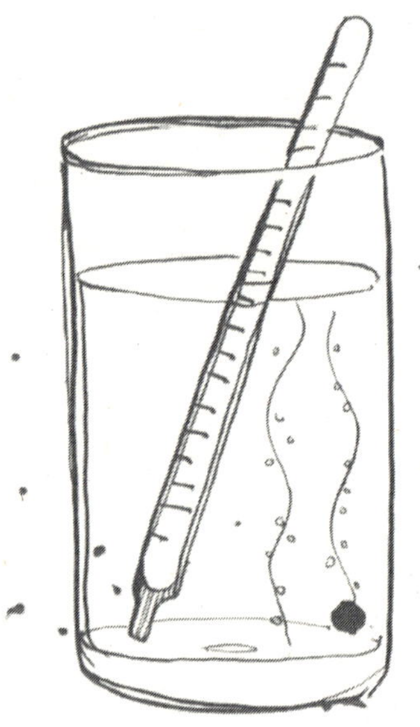

"Glucozade" was first manufactured in 1927 by William Owen, a chemist from Newcastle who had experimented for years trying to provide a pleasant-tasting, easy-digestible source of energy for those who were sick with common illnesses, like colds or the flu.

It initially became available throughout Britain for use in hospitals under the name Glucozade, packaged in glass bottles and covered in cellophane.

The name changed to Lucozade in 1929, and Beecham's acquired the product in 1938. By the early 1950s, Lucozade was available to everyone, and was the source of half of the company's profits.

During the 1950s, 1960s and 1970s, Lucozade used heavyweight national advertising support depicting how it 'aids recovery' and was the nicest part of being ill. One famous ad showed two mums discussing how it was better (quieter and easier) for them when their children were ill, but now that Lucozade had aided their recovery, the children were back to their noisy, boisterous selves.

As the 1980s arrived, as a result of increased advertising regulations and the desire to try and appeal to a broader audience, the brand was re-positioned as a drink to get you through "the ups and downs of the day". It wasn't a great success and the brand went into decline.

So it was in 1982 that the brand went through a second repositioning, a change that was to become one of the most famous in UK marketing history.

What the Lucozade team recognized was that the core of the brand was energy, not illness. So, together with advertising agency Ogilvy & Mather (O&M), they turned the brand's original positioning on its head – Lucozade wasn't energy for ill people, it was energy for well, fit people.

They needed a new brand 'spokesperson', and their choice was the complete opposite of the original sick child. It was Olympic decathlete (and soon to be gold medal winner and world record holder) Daley Thompson.

In place of the inane, bland pop tunes the brand had previously used, the first ad featuring Daley Thompson was accompanied by a high-energy song from heavy metal band Iron Maiden.

It showed Daley, a fit man in his prime, training hard and drinking Lucozade. In the era of new fitness regimes and the body beautiful (think Jane Fonda's *Workout* 1982 and Arnold Schwarzenegger in *Terminator* 1984), it was a timely move and the brand quickly went back into growth.

Between 1984 and 1989, UK sales tripled. The brand was certainly getting better.

And the moral is, a fresh perspective on your brand can help drive growth. How could you re-imagine what's at the core of your brand?

95. THE COWBOY AND THE RUBY LIPS

In the 1920s, one of the Philip Morris' leading brands of cigarettes was marketed to women as being as "mild as May". Another slogan used was "cherry tipped for your ruby lips" because the brand had a distinctive red band around the filter which helped hide any inelegant lipstick marks.

The ads featured stylish women posing in plush settings, often with a feminine hand reaching for a cigarette.

The brand was Marlborough. A name that could be traced back to the first Philip Morris factory in Great Marlborough Street, London.

During World War II, however, sales of the brand declined. Starting in the early 1950s, scientific data about the harmful effects of smoking began to emerge, and perhaps surprisingly this prompted Philip Morris to consider whether it could do more with its Marlborough brand.

The firm recognized it needed to shift its focus to filtered brands. But to succeed, it would need to overcome perceptions that filtered cigarettes, and especially brands like Marlborough, were cigarettes for women.

The new Marlborough brand would have to be a far cry from the old one. The first change Philip Morris made was the name, it was shortened to Marlboro. Along with the "ugh", out went the red band on the filter. Red was retained as part of a bold new geometric packaging design created by designer, Frank Gianninoto.

The biggest changes came in the advertising, where Philip Morris turned to Leo Burnett (advertising agency) to create a whole new image. The claims made in the new advertising reflected the new positioning as a safer, but still full flavoured, option …for men.

"Man-sized taste of honest tobacco comes full through. Smooth-drawing filter feels right in your mouth. Works fine but doesn't get in the way. Modern Flip-top box keeps every cigarette firm and fresh until you smoke it."

The striking new campaign was about as far away as you could get from the genteel saloons of the 1920s. The "new Marlboro smoker is a lean, relaxed outdoorsman – a cattle rancher, a navy officer, a flyer – whose tattooed wrist suggested a romantic past, a man who had once worked with his hands, who knew the score, who merited respect" reported *Esquire* magazine.

It was an image they felt projected "virility without vulgarity, quality without snobbery". It seemed America agreed with them: sales, which had been $5 billion in 1955, rose to $20 billion by 1957 – a 300% increase within two years.

In those first few years of the campaign, different types of "outdoorsmen" were shown, and the responses to each were carefully monitored. The cowboy emerged as the clear favourite, so the campaign soon focused on the contemplative cowboy enjoying his smoke in what was to become the familiar terrain of Marlboro County.

And the moral is, a brand can be repositioned to give itself a new lease of life. How could you reposition your (declining) brand?

96. WHEN THE BRICK MET THE FORCE

"Over my dead body" wasn't quite the response that Peter Eio had been hoping for.

It was early 1997, and after months of hard work and careful negotiation, Eio, who was chief of Lego's operations in the Americas, had just made his pitch to the group's senior management.

His proposal was that Lego should partner with Lucasfilm Ltd to bring out a licensed line of Lego *Star Wars* toys. The line would accompany the first instalment of the long-awaited *Star Wars* prequel trilogy, which was coming out in the spring of 1999.

However, while many people at Lucasfilm were AFOLs – Adult Fans Of Lego and loved the idea, the senior players in Lego's head office in Billund, Denmark, clearly weren't so keen.

"Normally the Danes are very polite people," recalled Eio. "We never had huge confrontations. But their initial reaction to *Star Wars* was one of shock and horror that we would even suggest such a thing. It wasn't the Lego way."

It was true that the deal would represent a significant change for Lego. Previously Lego had avoided partnerships and licensing deals, preferring to always go its own way. Lego already had space-themed kits.

"It was almost as if Lego didn't trust outside partners," said Eio. "The thinking was always, 'we'll do it ourselves. We can do it better.'"

Lego also continued to embrace one of founder Ole Kirk Christiansen's core values: never let war seem like child's play. The prospect of introducing attack cruisers, assassin droids, and other *Star Wars* armaments worried many of the senior team.

"The very name, *Star Wars*, was anathema to the Lego concept," Eio asserted. "It was just so horrid to them that we'd even consider linking with a brand that was all about battle."

Despite this resistance, Eio believed that his "battle" – no his "mission" – was to persuade the company to marry the Brick with the Force. For Eio, the most compelling reason to do a deal with Lucasfilm was the danger of not doing so.

Eio had seen how the United States was becoming a licence-driven market, and that hit movies and TV cartoon series were spinning off countless licensed products. By the mid-1990s, half of all toys sold in the United States were licensed. Key competitors, like Hasbro and Mattel, weren't avoiding deals but actively pursuing them with the likes of

Disney and Pixar. Eio feared that if Lego didn't tap into this shift in the market, it would fall helplessly behind.

Eio teamed up with Howard Roffman, Lucasfilm's licensing chief, and launched an internal campaign to convince the Lego group's senior executives that the *Star Wars* deal was a good one.

The first step was to ensure that Lego saw *Star Wars* as more Ivanhoe than GI Joe; that despite its futuristic space environment, at its heart it was a classic confrontation between good and evil, with little blood and no guts.

The next step was to involve the likely customers – Lego-buying parents. Together Eio and Roffman arranged a large survey of parents, not just in the United States, but in Germany, Lego's largest and most conservative market. Parents in the US overwhelmingly supported the idea; but more surprisingly, so did German parents.

Nevertheless, there was some continuing resistance to the *Star Wars* deal in Billund.

In the end, it came down to Kjeld Kirk Kristiansen, the CEO and grandson of the original founder. Encouraged by the poll results, and an ardent Star Wars fan himself, he overruled his more tradition-bound executives and gave the deal his vote. And what was to become one of the most successful partnerships in the toy industry's history finally got the go-ahead.

Launched to coincide with the release of *The Phantom Menace*, Lego *Star Wars* was a staggering hit, accounting for more than one-sixth of company sales.

And the moral is, co-branding (and licensing) can help give your brand a new lease of life. Who should you consider partnering with?

97. A STORY ABOUT STORYTELLERS WITH A STORYBOOK ENDING

About a decade ago, Disney Animation nearly came to a premature end. After a series of poorly performing films, the corporation was considering closing down its famous studio; instead it bought the newer kid on the block, who was on perhaps the hottest streak ever in animation – Pixar.

Now 10 years later, Disney is celebrating the success of *Frozen*, its highest-grossing animated film ever, and has already started work on *Frozen 2*.

Adopting Pixar's practice of a rapid sequel, like Toy Story 2, however, isn't the key idea that Disney has taken from Pixar. The Pixar practice that *is* being credited with turning Disney Animation around is its "story trust" – a process of collective constructive criticism.

During its development, a new film is screened up to seven times to an audience of Disney Animation employees who are free to give their opinions. The director and a 'trust' of 20 executives then meet off-site to consider and address the criticisms. The sessions generally last a day, but can be longer if the criticisms are numerous or fundamental to the storyline or characterization.

Andrew Millstein, head of the Disney Animation told *The Sunday Times* (29 March 2015): "It's a melee…But if you let your ego interfere, you're not going to get the most out of the process. The reason you're there is not to argue with what people see and whether it's working or not, but to listen to what's working or not."

Frozen went on this journey and made "seismic changes" along the way. At the start, Elsa and Anna weren't sisters, Elsa was the villain of the piece, there were no trolls, nor was there a Kristoff.

The use of "crit" sessions was originally adopted at Pixar as a means for the team of early pioneers of computer animation to learn from each other's successes and, just as importantly, each other's mistakes. Ed Catmull, one of those early team members and now president of Pixar Animation Studios, credits Toyota with helping to inspire the approach that encourages the whole team to catch mistakes before it is too late.

"In their car factories, everybody had a duty to find errors. Even the guys on the assembly line could pull the red cord and stop the line if they saw a problem. It wasn't just the job of the guys in charge. It was a group process. And so what happened at Toyota was a massive amount of incremental improvement. People on the production line constantly suggested lots of little fixes, and all those little fixes had a way of adding up to a quality product. That model was very influential for me as we set about figuring out how to structure the Pixar meetings."

That same philosophy, which helped Pixar, is now very influential at Disney Animation. It is helping it deliver quality product – great and highly successful animated films.

And the moral is, brands can benefit from constructive criticism. How do you ensure you hear and act on criticism (however painful)?

98. RYANAIR AND ITS ROAD TO DAMASCUS CONVERSION

The Ryanair brand was built on a business model of low fares, quick turn-around times for aircraft, "no frills", no business class and a single type of aircraft. It was supported by a simple and strictly applied approach to customer service model which Michael O'Leary, its outspoken chief executive, explained in an interview in *The Guardian* newspaper as "our customer service used to be fairly narrowly defined as the lowest fares, an on-time flight and we didn't lose your bag. But if it was anything more than that we would tell you politely to go away."

And for Michael O'Leary that is putting it politely – early utterances of his include the famous, "You're not getting a refund so f**k off. We don't want to hear your sob stories. What part of 'no refund' don't you understand?"

and

"People say the customer is always right, but you know what – they're not. Sometimes they are wrong and they need to be told so."

Implemented in 1992, these strategies helped transform a struggling and loss-making regional airline into one of Europe's most used and most profitable airlines in the course of 20 years. However, it also meant Ryanair got a reputation for being mean and completely unsympathetic.

But in 2013, the brand, and Michael O'Leary, had a 'road to Damascus' moment. The company saw a drop in profits, which may well have been the spur for change for them, but according to O'Leary, "We won the war in fares, there was no one left to compete with us on price. So, it was the logical thing to do, to go and compete with people on customer service and being nice."

O'Leary felt that the company needed "to improve and address the negatives that were previously associated with the Ryanair brand". So in the following year it started to change and got rid of a lot of the policies that passengers did not like, allowed more carry-on baggage and provided allocated seating, although this did involve increased charges.

Things have therefore started to get better for Ryanair customers. "We recognize we're not quite there yet. [But] passengers at primary airports trying us for the first time like the new policies, they like the friendly, smiley cabin crew and the feedback has been positive," O'Leary said.

And being nice seems to be paying off. There was a 32% jump in first-half profits a year after Ryanair's pledge to transform its customer service. Then Ryanair forecast its 2014 full-year profits after winter – traditionally a loss-making period – would be in the region of €750m to €770m, 45% higher than the prior year.

Complaints to Ryanair in 2014 were down 40% on 2013, to 80,000 letters a year.

The now converted Michael O'Leary said: "What we have been doing is significantly improving the customer service and it is working like a dream. The underlying trend is enormously positive. Since we changed the strategy, being fundamentally nicer to our customers, the business has boomed. If I had known being nicer to customers was going to work so well, I would have started many years ago."

And the moral is that brands need to evolve. How can you stimulate change while maintaining the core?

99. THE WELLINGTON REBOOTED

July 2006, and supermodel Kate Moss is photographed at the Glastonbury festival wearing a pair of black, chunky, knee-high rubber boots.

The photograph is seen by millions, many of whom probably thought "that woman could wear anything and still look good". But Michael Todd, who had previously worked with Ugg in Australia, thought something completely different. He thought "opportunity".

The boots in question were made by 150-year-old British brand – Hunter.

Todd decided to call Hunter's chief executive, Peter Mullen. Todd explained his thinking to Mullen. Moss' unprompted choice of a pair of traditional old Hunters, which wasn't a classic brand placement, meant the brand might be well positioned to shed its old-fashioned, even stuffy image. Todd's pitch was that the brand needed to be 're-booted' to target a younger, more fashion-conscious audience.

Mullen listened, and six months later hired Todd, making him the company's chief marketing officer and charging him with reinventing the Hunter brand.

In the past, Hunter had targeted its boots at British farmers, horse lovers and members of the "leisured" class who wore them while mucking out stalls and tending sheep. But its image was damaged when the company went into bankruptcy in 2005.

In April 2006, it was acquired by a consortium of owners, including Mullen – the founder of Thomas Pink shirt makers.

Todd decided that he wanted to play up the bootmaker's historic appeal, but that it should be, as he had suggested to Mullen, targeted at 'middle and upper class high-flyers' the sort of people who went "glamping" (glamourous camping) to festivals like Glastonbury.

In 2007, he persuaded a buyer at John Lewis to carry two styles of Hunter boots at its store in Reading, England, the site of another big annual music festival. It was to prove a turning point; the boots sold quickly, and today John Lewis sells 30 Hunter lines nationally.

Through his connections made at Ugg – another long-established brand that had become trendy among the fashion conscious – Todd secured mentions and features in magazines such as *Grazia* in the UK, and *Vogue* in the US, and soon even more "trendsetters" were seen wearing jeans and tights tucked inside their Hunter boots.

The brand had royal connections; in 1977 Prince Philip, Duke of Edinburgh, had awarded Hunter boots a Royal Warrant, which designated the company as an official supplier to the Royal Family.

With a new generation of aspirational royals – Prince William, Kate and Prince Harry – who were all part of the glamourous outdoor young country set, Todd decided it was time that the brand started playing up those associations. He made the Royal Warrant logo more prominent on the tags and packaging of Hunter boots. Todd is the first to explicitly recognize the benefit of the warrant and the fact that the princes did indeed wear Hunters: "We, as a brand, can capitalize on that."

In 2008, Hunter made $2.8 million pre-tax, a 25% increase over 2007 on sales that rose 60% to $22.7 million.

And the moral is, a new target audience can help rejuvenate an old brand. Who else could your brand be targeting?

100. SOMETIMES THE ANSWER IS IN FRONT OF YOUR EYES

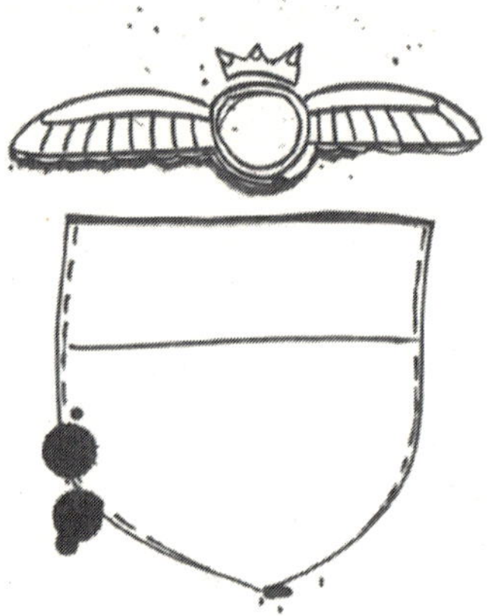

Kerris Bright likes a challenge, but even she admits that she thought twice before accepting the role as head of global marketing at British Airways.

"When I was thinking about joining British Airways, the company was losing a billion pounds a year, not a small sum of money. Customers were pretty dissatisfied and losing faith in the company, in its commitment to serving them well. It was a time of strikes. The colleagues in the organization were conflicted about why they existed and who they were serving. They were railing against that and against management."

In the end she saw, not the problem, but the opportunity. "If ever there was a time to try and reignite the kind of spirit that organization had had previously, and to get people to think and talk a little bit about why they exist, why they are there and what they care deeply about, this was the time to do it."

So, she began a project to revitalize the brand. Recognizing that the best brands come from within, she decided to work inside out. The programme started by giving staff the time to think and talk about their roles, and the reasons for believing in the brand. "What I found was that actually when people got the chance to talk, firstly they talked about their differences, such as the different ways they got into the business. But soon they found a unified reason why they wanted to be with that business and why they felt that airline was special."

What she and her team found was that "there was a deep commitment and passion for flying, that the business felt it understood and knew how to run an airline and fly people better than anybody else, and at the heart of everything it wanted to serve customers in a kind of uniquely special way".

What's more, "everybody felt this, but they had a slightly different view of how to articulate that".

The missing piece was, at least for a while, the expression of this passion. But the answer was in front of everyone's eyes, and it took a group of pilots to remind everyone what it was.

Kerris recalls: "They reminded us that written in their uniforms, on the side of the planes, on their caps it says 'To fly, To Serve'. Talking with them, they said actually this is why we exist. We know safety and security is important, but we exist 'to fly to serve'. So we decided as a marketing-led organization to make that our purpose. At this time of conflict and change, this was something that everyone could unify behind. We had started inside out, but now the organization felt really excitd, a bit proud and said yes, this is what we want to be, and then we started to bring that to life for customers."

And the moral is, sometimes brand archaeology is a good source of inspiration when looking to revitalize your brand. What in your brand's past could be brought back to life?

101. A TALE OF TWO STORES

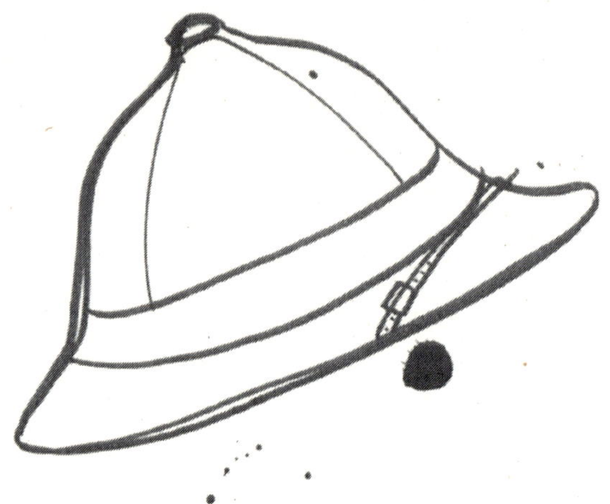

Once upon a time, there were two stores.

The first is sleek, chic and minimalist in design, with white walls and wooden parquet floors. It offers "modern, refined clothing and accessories for men and women… what you want to wear to work". The clothes are versatile, contemporary classics in styles that are both modern and (reasonably) timeless. Their aim is to "dress men and women who see every day as full of possibilities and seek to make the most of every moment and opportunity. We see life a little differently. We take it all in. We add to it. We make it our own and we live with style".

The second store is a little different. Life-size model giraffes and elephants stand amid old leather suitcases and wooden-crate racks piled with khaki "safari" clothing

– Ghurkha shorts, pith helmets and chamois shirts with deep cargo pockets. A World War II Army Jeep balances on top of some boulders in the front window and above the sales floor; an old bush plane hangs from the ceiling that has been painted to resemble a blue Zimbabwean sky. Safari and travel clothes include surplus military clothing customized with civilian touches like suede elbow patches, belts and wood buttons.

Lying around are distinctive catalogues. They contain no photos of the clothes, no models posing attractively; instead, they feature beautiful illustrations of the clothing, printed in soft duotone, alongside stories of far away places and the romance of travel.

The twist in the tale is that these two stores are in fact the same store, and if you haven't guessed the brand, they are both Banana Republic.

The second store is in fact the original store. It was set up by Mel and Patricia Ziegler, and opened its doors in 1978 in Mill Valley, California.

Mel and Patricia met when both worked at the *San Francisco Chronicle* (he as a photojournalist, she an illustrator). The couple both quit on the same day and went travelling. But it was Mel's search for a replacement for his well-worn and well-loved military surplus jacket that was to lead to the creation of the store. Ziegler finally found a British Burma jacket in a Sydney "disposal" store, which his wife altered to downplay the garment's military look and, according to Banana Republic's archives, "to play up its sensibility as a comfortable, utilitarian, everyday garment".

Family and friends admired the jacket's look, and this prompted the Zieglers to set up what was to become the Banana Republic Travel and Safari Clothing Company. While many Americans thought "surplus" meant only camouflage US Army T-shirts, they seemed to fall in love with the exotic military leftovers the Zieglers scrounged on their international buying trips.

"In England, we found Melton wool overcoats made for the British army selling for 25 bucks," Ziegler recalls. Banana Republic marketed the clothing as rare and marked it up. It made good business sense. "We weren't losing money."

By 1983, Banana Republic had five stores in California, a handful in other locations, and was bringing in $10 million a year. Don Fisher, who co-founded Gap made them an offer. It was an offer to buy them out, fund expansion but leave them in creative control. It was an offer that was simply too good to refuse, so they didn't.

For the next few years, things went well, riding on the back of films like *Out of Africa*, *Romancing the Stone* and the *Indiana Jones* series, the brand grew and grew. The Zieglers switched from selling adapted surplus clothing to using it as a template for manufacturing their own clothing.

However, the stock market crashed in 1987 and sales wobbled – the brand made a loss in 1988, Fisher worried about the future and indeed whether the safari fad had run its course. So, he brought in Mickey Drexler. Drexler, who would go on to help revive Gap, wasn't a fan of pith helmets and wanted to take Banana Republic in a more mainstream direction. He and the Zieglers clashed, and Mel and Patricia left citing the classic "fundamental creative and cultural differences".

Drexler brought in a new management team and, slowly at first and then with more momentum, the brand shifted its focus away from khaki to one that included brighter-coloured casual wear and cruise line apparel. In 1989, the catalogue was discontinued. Stores were refurbished to reflect a more sophisticated, modern, urban style.

The early 1990s saw a positive turn-around for Banana Republic when it further diversified its product lines, adding a variety of looks suitable for the office, and new advertising campaigns were adopted to sell the company's new relaxed, urban lifestyle image.

Nowadays it remains highly successful with over 600 stores around the world and a loyal young clientele, many of whom are too young to remember the original concept.

The brand, however, believes that life is still a journey, and plays to the notion of safari – only now its focus is the urban jungle. "Today, Banana Republic continues to outfit those on the modern journey of life. From harnessing the urban safari, to getting a promotion, to living out one's dreams, our customers will be perfectly dressed for every step of the way."

And the moral is that a brand needs to decide what is an enduring theme and what is a fad, so it can adapt accordingly. Is your brand relying on a fad or a long-term theme?

Footnote: The only question remaining is whether, given time, could the Zieglers have turned it around? Indeed speaking a few years ago, Mel Zielger said he ran into Fisher at a cocktail party and recalls that the Gap founder was repentant. "He came up to me and said he really regretted what he had done [to Banana Republic]." He went on to wonder what might have been "if we could wind back the clock, the challenge would have been for us to keep it fresh year after year. But they felt that we had taken a metaphor and gotten as much as we were going to get out of it".

THE MORALS

These stories don't really classify as fables as they feature real people (mostly), not animals (with the odd exception).

They do, however, each contain a moral and, while I wouldn't claim to be in the same league as Aesop (the Ancient Greek story teller), I would like to think that these stories provide more than just entertainment.

I hope they are informative, instructive and maybe even occasionally inspirational.

Brought together as they are in the next section, they are a toolbox of tips and techniques, which marketers can use when they consider some of the issues and challenges they face.

BRANDING

1. How Coca-Cola Took Over The World (Coca-Cola)
   Good PR can provide some of the most effective and cheapest publicity for your brand.
   What more could your brand do with PR?
2. Brownie Wise – The Queen Of Tupperware (Tupperware)
   Brands can drive change, not just in business but society too.
   What change is your brand driving?
3. Go On, Annoy Your Customers, It's Good For Business, It's Good For The World (Tony's)
   You can build your brand right into your products.
   How can your product or service tell your story for you?
4. A Road So Bad They Just Had To Buy It (VW)
   It pays to go to extreme lengths to test the quality of your brand.
   How far will you go to prove your brand?
5. The Brand Built On A Handshake (IMG)
   Brands are built on trust.
   What have you done to demonstrate you deserve the trust of your customers?
6. The Gangster, The Letter And The Dandy Car (Ford)
   The effects of good customer feedback can be multiplied through exploiting PR opportunities.
   How could you make more of your positive customer feedback?
7. Just A Smile And A Few Drops Of Chanel No 5 (Chanel)
   Celebrity endorsement can be a powerful tool to build your brand.
   Who and how would you like to endorse your brand?
8. Tell Them To Go And Do Something Else (Pintrest)
   The best brands realize that they are only a small part of their users' lives.
   How do you make sure you don't over-estimate the loyalty of your users?
9. Threadless Not Clueless, The Brand Inspiring Awesomeness (Threadless)
   The best brands build communities, not just customers.
   What are you doing to build a community around your brand?
10. Every Building Tells A Story (Disney)
    The best brands have a plan B.
    What will you do if your first plan doesn't succeed?
11. An Uncomfortable Vision (John Lewis)
    The best brands strive to deliver something other than shareholder value.
    What is the vision of your brand?
12. Naughtiness In The Noughties – What Happened When Virgin Turned 18 (Virgin)
    The best brands stay true to their core beliefs.
    What are the principles on which your brand rests (NB A principle isn't a principle until it costs you money)?
13. The Brand Is Mightier Than The Business (Blackwing 602)
    What can you do to ensure you maintain your brand's equity in the face of business issues?

14. Provoking An Emotional Response The Birds Eye Way (Birds Eye)
    Be careful which emotions you play with, you never know what might happen.
    What emotional responses do you want your brand to evoke?
15. The Insightful Bastard (Revlon)
    There is a big difference between a product and a brand.
    What is it that you are really selling?

ORIGINS

16. Third Time Lucky (Nespresso)
    Sometimes approaching an existing market in a new way can be better than trying to play in a new market by existing rules.
    How could you bend the rules in your existing market?
17. The Billion Dollar Butt (Spandex)
    It pays to truly believe in your brand.
    How far are you willing to go to help your brand succeed?
18. The Alligator Bag And The Polo Shirt (Lacoste)
    The best brands create distinctive personalities.
    How are you nurturing your brand's personality?
19. How Ben And Jerry Built Their Brand On A $5 Correspondence Course, A Social Conscience And a sense of humour (Ben & Jerry's)
    The best brands give something back to their communities.
    What is the right thing for your brand to be giving back?
20. He Knows About Toes (Christian Louboutin)
    It pays to make your brand truly distinctive.
    How do you ensure distinctiveness in your brand?
21. Johan's Satiable Curitosity (Peppadew)
    Sometimes a good idea is sitting right in front of you.
    What is so obvious that you might have missed it?
22. The Optometrist And The Nationalist (Fazer Blue)
    Visual clues can be stronger than written ones
    What could you say better in images and colours than in words?
23. The Colonel, The Secret Recipe And The 600 Handshakes (KFC)
    The best brands can be built on a variety of business systems.
    Is there a new business model that could transform your brand?
24. Heads Or Tails (Benefit)
    Every brand needs a little luck... but you need to use it when you get it.
    Have you recently had a piece of good fortune and have you exploited it?
25. A Man Of Vision, Perseverance And Curiosity (Birds Eye)
    Great brands can be built on vision, curiosity and perseverance.
    Have you got these three qualities in your brand team?
26. Murder Most Profitable (Clue/Cluedo)
    Brands can be built on 'imaginative notions'.
    Where will your brand find some new 'imaginative notions'?

27. A Fashion Fairy Tale, A Marketing Master Class (Diane Von Fürstenberg)
    Brands can be built on consumer understanding.
    How well do you understand the lives and motivations of your consumer?
28. All Wrapped Up (Hallmark)
    Sometimes necessity can be the mother of invention.
    What opportunities can you find in any moments of adversity you face?
29. Salesmanship Down To A Tea (Lipton)
    If people don't know about your brand, how will they know whether or not to buy it? How can you ensure maximum publicity for your brand?
30. How A Russian Helped Create An American Brand Icon (Levi's)
    Innovation in one market often borrows from other markets.
    Where could you borrow ideas from?
31. How An Over-Worked Baker, The US Navy And The Executive's Wife Helped Create The Greatest kitchen aid ever (KitchenAid)
    A brand can be built on solving people's problems.
    What problems do you know that haven't been solved yet (or could be solved better)?
32. Napoleon, Two Mathematically Minded Ministers And The Birth Of The Insurance Funds Industry (Scottish Widows)
    A brand may have a noble purpose but needs a sensible business model to succeed.
    How strong is your brand's underlying business model?
33. How A Standard Lamp Inspired One Of The Fastest Growing Online Fashion Brands
    Inspiration for a new brand can come from anywhere at any time.
    Do you have your eyes and ears working 24/7?
34. R A L S B E B C = 14 at least (Scrabble)
    Not all successful brands are overnight sensations.
    Are you giving your new brands enough time?
35. Absolutely Fabulis? No. Fabulously Fab, Absolutely! – How Two Wrongs Led To A Right (Fabulis)
    Sometimes you need to admit your first idea wasn't right and needs to be adapted.
    Do you learn from mistakes and make necessary changes?
36. Teach Yourself – The Redbus Story (Redbus)
    If you want create something new, you need to be willing to learn new skills.
    Are your ideas being held back because you are too set in your ways?
37. The Best Job In The World (Hotel Chocolat)
    Brands can be built by turning a passion into a purpose.
    How could your passion become the basis for a new brand?

NAMING & IDENTITIES

38. Introducing Miss White From London (Hello Kitty)
    A brand can benefit from a backstory.
    What is the story behind your brand?

39. When Dark And Broken (Coca Cola)
    Packaging can be your silent salesman.
    Are you doing enough with your packaging?
40. A Roaring Success (MGM)
    The best brand identities can live on and on if constantly updated.
    Is your brand identity strong enough to stand the test of time?
41. The Swallow, The Steamships And The Jaguar (Jaguar)
    Some of the best brand names are associative.
    How will you choose the name for your next new launch?
42. The Spirit Of The Blitz Bottled (London Pride)
    Brand names can come from anywhere including your customers.
    How will you develop your next new brand name?
43. Big, Green And Not Very Jolly (Big Green Giant)
    Literal translations of brand names into icons don't always work, sometimes you need some creative licence.
    How can you adapt your logo to make it more engaging and appealing?
44. Can A Blue Box Make A Woman's Heart Beat Faster? (Tiffany)
    Brands can own colours and their associations in their customers' minds.
    What colour would you like to own for your brand and why?
45. The Strangest Brand Icon In The World (Lyle)
    The best designs don't just identify, they signify something.
    Does your brand design do more than just identify it as your brand?
46. Taking His Daughter's Name (Mercedes)
    Sometimes brand names need a while before they are fully accepted.
    Have you been too hasty in your judgment of brand names?
47. Any Colour You Want As Long As It's Black (And White) (WWF)
    A tight creative brief is often the best brief.
    Are you doing everything to make sure your brief is clear and concise?
48. Maybe It Will Grow On Me (Nike)
    Sometimes brand identities need a while before they are fully accepted.
    Have you been too hasty in your judgment of brand identities?
49. The Banker, The Stationer And The Engineer (Mont Blanc)
    A brand identity can be expressed in many forms across different media.
    How could you further develop your brand's communication equities?
50. No Ordinary Whisky, No Ordinary Name (Monkey Shoulder)
    Your product history can be an inspiration for a new brand name.
    Can you look back to find a name for the future?

MARKETING STRATEGY

51. The Ladder To Success (General Motors)
    Balancing economies of production with a selectively tailored offer is at the heart of marketing segmentation.
    How can you segment your market to your advantage?

52. When Less Was More (Apple)
    (As Steve Jobs said) Deciding what not to do is as important as deciding what to do. What should you be saying 'no' to?
53. A Stellar Approach To Selling Tyres (Michelin)
    Promotional items can add value in their own right.
    Can you monetize any of your promotional items?
54. A Bird In The Air Is Worth A Book In The Hand (Guinness World Records)
    You never know when a business opportunity will arise.
    Are your ears and eyes open to opportunity 24/7?
55. Wake Up And (Don't) Smell The Coffee (Starbucks)
    Short-term growth isn't everything.
    Are you staying true to your brand's core values?
56. The Salesman In Basketball's Hall Of Fame (Converse)
    The best celebrity endorsements are much more than advocacy.
    Are you using any celebrity endorsements you have to maximum mutual effect?
57. A Valentine's Romance – When Ken Met Barbie (Barbie)
    Creating content is a powerful means of building engagement with your brand.
    Are you creating the content around your brand?
58. Don't Mention The… Lady Days (Kotex)
    It is easy to forget how important being on display – mental availability – is.
    What are you doing to maximize your mental availability?
59. The (W)Hole Story (Lifesavers)
    If you are a seasonal product it is worth exploring opportunities across the year.
    How can you extend the usage of your brand?
60. The Original Incredibles (Boeing)
    The best brands transfer learning across their business units.
    What learning should you be sharing further?
61. Zigging When The World Is Zagging (LinkedIn)
    There are opportunities in being the same but different.
    How can you find a new angle in an existing market space?
62. Pamela Anderson, The Sherman Tank And The Failed Invasion Of America (Virgin Cola)
    It pays to pick your battles carefully.
    Are you sure you can win your must-win battles?
63. With Friends Like These (Walkers)
    Sometimes your competition will be on your own doorstep.
    How do you ensure you are your company's best option?
64. It's Not A Problem, It's An Opportunity (Corona)
    Good brands can turn a problem into an opportunity.
    What problem could you use to your advantage?
65. Friends In High Places (The Jelly Belly Candy Company)
    Friends in high places and in the public spotlight are friends indeed and are worth cultivating.

Which famous person could be a brand advocate for you?

66. From Bags To Riches (Lakeland)
    The best brands understand and look after their customers.
    What do you do to truly look after your customers?
67. How A Punk And A Dwarf Changed The Brewing World (Brewdog)
    New brands may need to start a revolution, not just a business.
    What revolution do you want your brand to lead?
68. From Toothpaste To Global Electronics - Lucky By Name But Brave And Bold In Deed (LG)
    The best brands dream big and set themselves audacious goals.
    What could you do if you stretched your thinking?

COMMUNICATION

69. Santa Claus And The Backwards Belt (Coca-Cola)
    You don't have to be first to market – size, spend and commitment can be more important. Where could you still win even if you aren't first to market?
70. A Tagline Is Forever (De Beers)
    Don't underestimate the power of an idea.
    Is there a big idea that can drive your brand to greater success?
71. The Tic Tac Toe Challenge (Kit Kat And Oreo)
    Your brand can benefit when it shows it's more than a business.
    How can you demonstrate that your brand has a human face?
72. The No-Sell Sell (Ronseal)
    Sometimes the best sell is no sell at all.
    Do you know what sort of approach works best with your target audiences?
73. Advertising Can Be A Force For Good (King Khalid Foundation)
    Advertising can be a force for good.
    How can you use communication to help drive both commercial and social issues?
74. Some Decisions Are Only For The Brave (SC Johnson)
    It can pay to be brave.
    What act of bravery could put your brand on the map?
75. If You Pay For Half I'll Pay For The Other Half (Apple)
    Great advertising is sometimes a leap of faith.
    Are you willing to follow your instincts?
76. The Men In The Hathaway Shirts – Part One: David Oglivy (Hathaway)
    Creative ideas can be borrowed from anywhere.
    Where will you find your next idea?
77. The Men In The Hathaway Shirts – Part Two: Ellerton Jette (Hathaway)
    The best propositions are based on a real understanding of the underlying needs and motivations of your target audience.
    How do you dig deeper with your research and understanding of your target audiences?

78. Dutch Courage (Unox)
The best brands integrate themselves into the community and seasonal occasions.
What opportunities exist for your brand to get closer to its local community?
79. Refreshing The Advertising – Hit Or Myth (Heineken)
Research provides information and insights that should guide decision-making, not replace it.
How have you been using research?

INNOVATION

80. When Armand Met Octave (Le Creuset)
The best innovations have distinctive equities built into them.
What equities can you create to integrate within your next innovation?
81. 11 Pages Short (National Geographic)
Sometimes inspiration strikes when you need it most.
How can you look at your next problem as an opportunity?
82. Red Thai At Night, Dietrich's Delight (Red Bull)
Good ideas travel well.
What could you take from elsewhere in the world and bring to your market?
83. Why Researchers Tricked A Woman Into Cleaning Her Floor (Swiffer)
Innovation is born by identifying a problem others hadn't seen before, and sometimes persevering and adapting the research approach until you find it.
How can you create a tailored research approach to help identify innovation opportunities?
84. The Pen For Readers Not Writers (Stabilo Boss)
Great design can create innovative new brands.
How can you use design to deliver a new or different benefit?
85. The Spitfire, The Umbrella And The Baby Buggy – A Story Of Cross Pollination (Maclaren)
Cross pollination of ideas is a great source of innovation.
Keep your eyes open to ideas from afar.
86. A Rubbish Idea (Frisbee)
One person's cast-off can be another's inspiration.
Have you ever looked at what you do from a completely different perspective?
87. Blue Sky Drinking (Cobra)
There is often opportunity sitting in the gaps between existing sectors.
Are there gaps between sectors you compete in?
88. A Family Obsession – Spreading A Little Luxury? (Nutella)
Brands can add value to commodities.
Do you have access to a plentiful commodity to which you could add value?
89. How Peugeot Found Success With A Detour Via The Kitchen Table (Peugeot)
Technical specialism can be the basis for a wide range of innovations.
Do you have a technical expertise that could be leveraged into another market?

90. Have You Heard The One About The Peddler, The Jeweller And The Attorney? (Brillo)
Innovation is often the result of mixing different skills and competencies to create something new.
What competencies could you mix up to create something new?
91. Diabetes And A Patio – The Story Behind The Story (No-Cal Cola And Diet Pepsi)
You don't have to be first to market to succeed.
Can you be a late entrant into an existing market and still win?
92. The Unhelpful Client (Duchy Originals)
You may need to try again before you succeed.
What idea do you have that deserves a second chance?
93. Music On The Move – Thanks To The Opera-Loving Chairman (Sony Walkman)
Occasionally what the chairman wants personally might just be what the market wants?
Do you have a personal passion that could be a winner?

REPOSITIONING AND RENNOVATION

94. The Brand That Got Better (Lucozade)
A fresh perspective on your brand can help drive growth.
How could you re-imagine what's at the core of your brand?
95. The Cowboy And The Ruby Lips (Marlboro)
A brand can be repositioned to give itself a new lease of life.
How could you reposition your (declining) brand?
96. When The Brick Met The Force (Lego & Star Wars)
Co-branding (and licensing) can help give your brand a new lease of life.
Who should you consider partnering with?
97. A Story About Storytellers With A Storybook Ending (Disney)
Brands can benefit from constructive criticism.
How do you ensure you hear and act on criticism (however painful)?
98. Ryanair And Its Road To Damascus Conversion (Ryanair)
Brands need to evolve.
How can you stimulate change while maintaining the core?
99. The Wellington Rebooted (Hunter)
A new target audience can help rejuvenate an old brand.
Who else could your brand be targeting?
100. Sometimes the answer is right in front of your eyes (British Airways)
Sometimes brand archaeology is a good source of inspiration when looking to revitalize your brand.
What in your brand's past could be brought back to life?
101. A tale of two stores (Banana Republic)
A brand needs to decide what is an enduring theme and what is a fad, so they can adapt accordingly.
Is your brand relying on a fad or a long-term theme?

FINAL WORDS

There are lots of good books on the theory of storytelling, which contain practical tips and guidance on how and why you should tell stories. How stories are more engaging and more memorable. How you should structure the plot and create characters. How you can use linguistic tools like the 'power of three'.

This book was never meant to compete with them or play that role; rather I wanted to tell stories. I wanted to complement those other books.

If you'll excuse some poetic licence, I wanted to be a minstrel for marketing or the bard of branding, entertaining and educating along the way – though I can't sing and my poetry is pretty poor too.

But like the bards and minstrels of old, I'm always on the look-out for more tales, so if you have one to share, let me know.

giles.lury@thevalueengineers.com